3RD EDITION

50 POWERFUL IDEAS YOU CAN USE TO KEEP YOUR CUSTOMERS

By
Paul R. Timm, Ph.D.

CAREER
PRESS
Franklin Lakes, NJ

**50 POWERFUL IDEAS YOU CAN USE TO KEEP YOUR CUSTOMERS
3RD EDITION**
Edited by Dianna Walsh
Typeset by Butch Myers
Cover design by Mada Design, Inc./NYC
Printed in the U.S.A. by Book-mart Press

To order this title, please call toll-free 1-800-CAREER-1 (NJ and Canada: 201-848-0310) to order using VISA or MasterCard, or for further information on books from Career Press.

CAREER
PRESS

The Career Press, Inc., 3 Tice Road, PO Box 687
Franklin Lakes, NJ 07417
www.careerpress.com

Library of Congress Cataloging-in-Publication Data

Timm, Paul R.
    50 powerful ideas you can use to keep your customers / by Paul R. Timm.—
3rd ed.
      p. cm.
    Includes bibliographical references (p.) and index.
    ISBN 1-56414-599-9 (pbk.)
      1.Customer services—Management. 2. Consumer satisfaction. 3. Supervision of employees. I. Title: Fifty powerful ideas you can use to keep your customers. II. Title.

HF5415.5 .T498 2002
658.8'12—dc   212001054396

CONTENTS

Since publishing the first edition of *50 Powerful Ideas* in 1992, the challenges of keeping customers and creating customer loyalty have become even more urgent. The economic good times of the 1990s have given way to a bumpy ride in the early 2000s. The dot-com boom and bust has reminded us all that businesses cannot thrive on a good idea alone. The experts are coming to realize that there is no distinction between "e-business" or "e-commerce" and just plain business or commerce. Ultimately, every successful enterprise must attract, serve, and win the loyalty of customers by providing worthwhile products and delivering excellent service.

I am increasingly convinced that getting and maintaining loyal customers affects an organization's bottom line more than any ad campaign, marketing program, or Public Relations effort. Turned-off customers produce devastating ripple effects that quickly drag companies into a morass of mediocrity while organizations that creatively apply a constant flow of small, customer-centered innovations see consistent and persistent strengthening of their customer base.

This book is designed to get all employees thinking about the little things that can make all the difference. If everyone in an organization improves awareness of the simple yet powerful ideas in this small volume, the company can and will see dramatic improvements in service and customer loyalty. The impact on the bottom line will be dramatic.

The Nature of Service Today

Have you ever had a poor customer service experience? Silly question, right? Everyone has faced rude or unhelpful people, bought products that disappoint, or had other unpleasant episodes as a customer. Poor service is an all-too-frequent experience for us all.

Some generally accepted facts about the impact of poor service point to the need for the skills that produce happy, loyal customers. (These statistics may not be precise numbers for your business, but they offer a thought-provoking insight into the importance of every customer as an individual.)

- Dissatisfied customers tell an average of 10 to 20 other people about their bad experience. Some, especially in the digital age of easy communication, tell far more.

- The cost of attracting a new customer is at least five times more than the cost of keeping an existing one.

- Up to 93 percent of dissatisfied customers will not buy from you again (if they have a choice)—and *they won't tell you why!*

- Some 96 percent of dissatisfied customers *do not complain* to a company about poor service. Instead they will simply go to a competitor. Yet 95 percent of dissatisfied customers will become loyal customers again if their complaints are handled well and quickly.

- With many businesses selling the same or similar products or services, quality of service is the only variable that can distinguish the company from its competition.

- Providing the kind of service that builds customer loyalty can increase profits, reduce costs, and lead to increased employee productivity.

- Customers are willing to pay more to receive better service.

GOOD NEWS AND BAD NEWS . . .

Customer satisfaction is like an election held everyday, and the people vote with their feet. If dissatisfied, they walk (sometimes run) to your competitor.

FIRST, THE BAD NEWS.

The typical company will lose 10 percent to 30 percent of its customers this year, mostly because of poor service. When customers have a choice, they'll go to the competition almost one third of the time.

When your customers don't have a choice—they are stuck with you because you are a public utility, government agency, or the only game in town—they'll use their feet for something else: they'll kick you. Customer dissatisfaction will erupt in the form of animosity directed toward you and your organization. Public relations efforts alone will provide little more than a bandage. The psychological toll on employees will result in higher turnover and additional costs as these burned-out workers need to be retrained or replaced.

NOW THE GOOD NEWS.

Organizations that initiate effective customer loyalty efforts have seen profits jump 25 to 100 percent. Monopoly or not-for-profit groups see reduced turnover, better financial results, and happier staffs.

Like it or not, customer service is the competitive battleground for the 21st century. In fact, it will always be the decisive battleground.

Most people accept, or at least give lip service to, the idea that "the customer is the boss." We talk about the customer "always being right." We say that the customer is "our reason for existing" as an organization. But the real management challenge lies in translating these slogans into actions that convey these feelings and beliefs into actions perceived by *customers*.

And even when leaders truly believe in the importance of customer service, they still face the difficulty of getting the customer-contact people to do what customers want. The problem gets trickier when we see that the lowest paid and least well-trained employees are often those who face the customer every day.

- A multibillion-dollar fast food operation, for example, places its success squarely in the hands of the minimum-wage teenager taking the orders and delivering the food.

- The image of a multibillion-dollar bank is created in the mind of the customer by the entry-level teller who handles his day-to-day transactions.

- A multibillion-dollar government agency is judged largely by the receptionist who answers the phone or greets the customer, thus setting a tone for any transaction. Many a criticism of the "government bureaucracy" can be traced to the attitudes of a receptionist. An otherwise pleasant transaction can be poisoned by "getting off on the wrong foot."

BUILDING CUSTOMER LOYALTY IS EVERYONE'S JOB

Regardless of your job title, position in an organization, or experience, *your number-one task* will *always* be to attract, satisfy, and preserve "customers." And *everyone has customers*. This book offers simple yet powerful ideas that will help you build competitive advantage through excellent service. The specific tips are easy to apply. And they'll get results.

7 STRATEGIES PROVIDE THE KEYS TO CUSTOMER LOYALTY

This book provides a workable framework for implementing ongoing processes that can build customer loyalty. To do so, companies need to focus on seven strategic areas.

They need to:

 1. Understand the **opportunities** in building customer loyalty.

 2. Identify customer **turnoffs**.

 3. **Recover** dissatisfied customers.

 4. Give customers exceptional **value**.

 5. Give customers better **information**.

 6. Show customers a positive and pleasant **personality**.

 7. Make customer experiences **convenient**.

The tips and ideas in this book show ways to implement such strategies. Each tip displays an icon that refers back to these key strategies.

PART I

POWERFUL IDEAS
THAT GET YOU FOCUSED

Too many organizations pay lip service to the need for great customer service but fail to get a clear focus on what is needed to build ongoing loyalty. Customer loyalty should be the major goal. In this section, we will discuss ideas about getting a clear focus.

IDEA 1.
UNDERSTAND THE GOAL OF CUSTOMER
LOYALTY.

Everyone in the organization needs to be clear about the goal of customer loyalty. Excellent service leads to customer satisfaction and that satisfaction is a critical element in creating customer loyalty. Loyalty is the ultimate goal.

Is loyalty the same thing as customer satisfaction or service? Not quite. Loyalty is a broader concept.

Customer loyalty is a concept that includes five factors:

1. The *overall satisfaction* customers experience when doing business with you.

2. The willingness to build a *relationship* with you and your company.

3. The willingness to be a *repeat buyer.*

4. The willingness to *recommend you to others.*

5. A *resistance to switching* to a competitor.

Customer loyalty is not the same as:

- *Customer satisfaction alone.* Although an important part of loyalty, today's satisfaction alone is no guarantee of future loyalty.

- *A response to some trial offer or incentive.* You cannot buy loyalty; you must earn it over time.

- *A large share of the market.* You may have a big customer base only because your competitors are weak or your pricing is better. These alone will not create loyalty.

- *Repeat buying alone.* Some people buy out of habit, convenience, or price but would be quick to defect to an alternative.

Be sure that you and all employees understand what it means to create a loyal customer. If we fail to have goal clarity, its achievement is unlikely.

IDEA 2.
RECOGNIZE WHAT TURNS OFF YOUR CUSTOMERS

Research in customer service repeatedly indicates that 60-70 percent of lost customers leave because of problems other than product quality or price. They get frustrated by the experience of doing business with the company; they feel they are not valued.

Get a few people together and ask them to describe some pet peeves about their experiences as customers and you'll get some very emotional reactions. Everyone can recall situations where they were treated poorly, inconvenienced, or bought products that just didn't measure up.

THREE CATEGORIES OF CUSTOMER TURNOFFS

The *customer turnoffs* that trigger negative emotions and cause dissatisfaction arise from three categories: value, systems, and people.

Value Turnoffs

Customers are turned off when they receive poor *value* from a shoddy product or sloppy work.

Value is defined as *quality relative to price paid.* If you purchase an inexpensive, throw-away item at a discount store—say a 79-cent pen—you may not be upset if it doesn't last very long. But buy a $79 fountain pen that leaks in your shirt pocket and you're furious. The purchase of an automobile, appliance, or professional service that quits working or fails to meet your needs will create a value turnoff.

Systems Turnoffs

The term *systems* is used to describe any *process, proce-dure, or policy used to "deliver" the product or service to the customer.* Systems are the way we get the value to the customer. Systems will include such things as:

- Employee training and staffing.
- Company location, layout, parking facilities, and phone lines.
- Record keeping (including computer systems for handling customer transactions).
- Policies regarding guarantees, returns, and so forth.
- Delivery or pick-up services.
- Marketing and sales policies.
- Customer follow-up procedures, and so on.

When a company does a poor job in any of these system areas it creates unhappy customers.

People Turnoffs

People turnoffs arise when employees fail to communicate well, both verbally (with words) and non-verbally (without words). Some examples of people turnoffs are:

- Failure to greet or even smile at a customer.
- Inaccurate information given or lack of knowledge conveyed.
- Talking to another employee or allowing telephone interruptions while ignoring a customer.
- Rude or uncaring attitude.
- High-pressure sales tactics.
- Inappropriate, dirty, or sloppy appearance (of the employee or the work location).
- Any communicated message that causes the customer to feel uncomfortable.

IDEA 3.
GATHER FEEDBACK AND APPLY SERVICE
RECOVERY SKILLS.

Knowing the sources of customer turnoffs is helpful as we try to minimize them. But, realistically, we can't always predict customer reactions.

Any company can give adequate customer service when everything goes well. A smooth transaction is easy. But when glitches occur—when customers have problems or are even a little bit disappointed—the great companies quickly distinguish themselves.

Customers react to you on the basis of their individual perceptions. What turns one customer off may have no effect on others. So, despite the best efforts of customer-savvy people, turnoffs inevitably arise. Problem situations should not be viewed as tragic, but as opportunities to further solidify customer loyalty.

Service recovery, of course, requires that we know when a customer is unhappy, and that requires feedback. We can receive a steady flow of customer feedback if we create a receptive relationship. But if you ask for feedback, be ready to act upon. Keep in mind these key facts about the feedback process:

1. When you ask people for their input (including comments and complaints), you increase their expectation that you will change in positive ways.

2. If you receive feedback and then fail to change for the better, you will cause customers to perceive you more negatively than if you had not received the feedback.

3. You can safely assume that all perceptions are real, at least to those who own them.

4. You will tend to be defensive. You might interpret some comments as insulting or abusive. In those cases, you will tend to denounce not only what was said but those who say it.

5. You will get more benefit from negative feedback than from receiving no feedback at all.[1]

Ignoring customers is a formula for disaster. Instead, focus on knowing how to discover and recover (win back) the unhappy customer. The payoff for recovering a potentially lost customer is actually an *increased* likelihood that he or she will be loyal to you. It sounds strange, but here is what researchers have found.

SURPRISING FACTS ABOUT DISSATISFIED CUSTOMERS

Surveys by the U.S. Office of Consumer Affairs reveal these interesting facts:

- One customer in four is dissatisfied with some aspect of a typical transaction.

- Only 5 percent of dissatisfied customers complain to the company. The vast silent majority would rather switch than fight. They simply take their business elsewhere.

- A dissatisfied customer will tell 10 to 20 other people (12 is the average) about a company that provided poor service. Some people will tell hundreds or even thousands.

Let's think about these statistics. If 25 percent of customers are unhappy with a company's service but only 5 percent of that 25 percent bother to complain (yet each unhappy customer tells a dozen others) the impact can be devastating. For simplicity, let's say a company serves 100 customers per day. Twenty-five of them are dissatisfied but the company hears only one or two complaints. That may sound good to management until they realize that the 23 quiet ones are likely to tell 274 other people about the unsatisfactory service!

Employees who recover one or two complaining customers may be saving a dozen others. Handling complaints from two or three dissatisfied people can save 30 or 40 possible defections. And it can teach the company what it needs to know to improve.

Further good news for companies that learn to effectively solicit and handle complaints is that such companies can charge an average of 8 to 15 percent more than their competitors, even in businesses where competition is keen. For example, Maytag, the quality home appliance maker with the "lonely repairman" campaign, supports a premium-priced product in a highly price-sensitive market.

The best news of all is that customers who have their complaints handled well are very likely to do business with the company again. While only 9 to 37 percent of dissatisfied customers who don't complain report a willingness to do business with the same company again, fully 50 to 80 percent of those whose complaints are fully resolved will consider doing repeat business, even if their complaints were not resolved in their favor.[2] Other findings put this number even higher.

That's the key fact to remember: Customers who complain and have their problem addressed are more likely to become loyal, even more likely than customers who never have a problem.

The task at hand, then, is to recognize (and help your employees see) that a complaining customer can be your company's best friend. But to save them you have to hear from them. So, enlightened companies work to boost the number of complainers they hear from.

The two steps needed to use this information, then, are:

1. Make it easy for your customers to complain.
2. Act upon such complaints quickly and efficiently.

Successful handling of customer complaints can solidify customer loyalty and be a gold mine of repeat business. Remember that formerly dissatisfied customers are more likely to be repeat buyers if you discover and recover them. I talk more about specific recovery techniques throughout this book. Look especially at the Ideas that have this icon: ☺.

IDEA 4.

KNOW HOW TO TELL WHEN YOU ARE TURNING OFF CUSTOMERS.

We all like to think we do a pretty good job at service, but the fact is we are constantly turning customers off. It's certainly not intentional, but it happens every day, and we need to be alert to the problem.

How can you tell when you are turning customers off? The short answer is to put yourself in the shoes of your customer. Objectively assess the way they are treated and compare this with how other companies may be treating them. As Yogi Berra said, "You can observe a lot by just watching."

While companies can use many ways of gathering feedback data (focus groups, surveys, and so on), perhaps the one most important thing that all employees can do is to simply listen to customers.

Few people are really good listeners, but those who are get a lot of good information. Listening is not a passive activity—something you "sit back" and do when you are not talking. Good listening requires active mental work.

To be a better listener, use these ideas:

- Judge the content of what people are saying, not the way they are saying it. Customers may not have the "right" words, but they know what they need. Listen beyond their tone of voice or their inability to articulate exactly what they want.

- Hold your fire. Don't jump to make judgments before your customer has finished talking. If he's upset, don't respond defensively. Just hear him out.

- Work at listening. Maintain eye contact and discipline yourself to listen to what is being said. Tune out any distracting thoughts. Make the customer the center of your attention.

- Seek clarification from customers so you fully understand their needs. Do this in a non-threatening way using sincere questions. Don't interrogate, but do ask them to help you understand what they mean. (Actually using the phrase, "help me to understand," can be an effective way to show your concern and get clarification.)

Listening and establishing understanding is the first step to earning customer loyalty.

IDEA 5.
KNOW WHO ALL YOUR CUSTOMERS ARE.

This may seem like strange advice. Obviously you know who your customers are. Or do you?

Customers. For many of us, these are easy to identify. They buy something or from us. But some people will say, "I don't work directly with customers." Before you accept this idea, I suggest a closer look at just who exactly your customers are. In organizations, customers take two forms: *internal* and *external*.

INTERNAL AND EXTERNAL CUSTOMERS

Internal customers are those people, departments, or organizations served by what we do. The only person who might have no internal customers is the individual who works completely alone and for himself. The rest of us all have at least one internal customer: our boss. As managers, we also have internal customers in the form of the people we supervise. They rely on us to meet their needs. Internal customers are a fact of life.

For example, a word-processing clerk or copy-center worker within a company serves other workers' needs for documents handling for the larger organizations. Personnel office staff serves employees' needs for benefits information, management's needs for staffing, and company needs for handling various government paperwork requirements.

"Happy employees equal happy customers equal happy stockholders," according to Jonah Keri of *Investor's Business Daily*. Identifying turnarounds in companies like Continental Airlines and several mutual fund companies, Keri makes a compelling case for the idea that employee satisfaction and company profits fly hand in hand. Before the turnaround, Continental employees had managers yelling at them, and pilots, flight attendants, and mechanics all sniping at each other, while top management sat in its ivory tower at corporate headquarters. Continental's customer satisfaction mirrored the dissatisfaction among its employees. But when management sought a turnaround, they started with efforts to boost employee satisfaction and all the organizational systems improved, including customer satisfaction.[3]

Internal customers are important. In fact, some enlightened companies measure their customer effectiveness by measuring employee satisfaction. If the employees are happy and engaged in positive ways, it automatically follows that the customers are being well served.

From your own experience, don't you prefer doing business where people seem to be having a good time?

External customers are those people or departments who are the end users of our organization's product or services. This is, of course, the traditional use of the term customer.

Often we call these people different names depending on our business: We call them customers, clients, guests, patients, patrons, cases, franchisees, passengers, students, and the like.

To keep things simple, this book will use the generic term "customer" throughout. But please bear in mind that you probably serve a number of different types of customers and you may call them something different.

A satisfied customer is one who purchases (although not always for money) and receives value from the goods and services you offer. Generally these customers have a choice. If they don't like what you offer or the way you offer it, they can go elsewhere for similar goods or services. When they do, you and your organization suffer. Satisfied customers create profits. Profits, in turn, create organizational success and the ability to pay employees.

Some organizations, however, have "captive customers." They provide a service customers can't get elsewhere. A public utility or a government agency are examples. Customers can't shop around for electric power or license plates. This brings up the question, *Why give good service if the customer has no choice but to deal with you?*

It's easy to see how keeping customers happy is important to the health of for-profit organizations, but why be so concerned with service in non-profit, monopolistic, or government agencies? After all, where else will they buy what we sell? Here's why:

In the government agency, public utility, or non-profit organization, customer displeasure with service quickly becomes customer animosity. This animosity can snowball. As customers come to expect that they're going to be treated poorly, they in fact will begin to treat the employee poorly (in "self-defense"). The attacked employee fights back and the stress on both parties mounts.

Some results of this stress on employees and the organization include:

- Increased stress-related illness.
- Employee burnout and absenteeism.
- Higher turnover—people quit.
- Cost and inconvenience of training replacement employees.
- Increased difficulty in attracting good employees to the job.
- Negative public view of the organization.
- Lower sense of pride in organization.
- Lower sense of self-worth among employees.
- Increased defensiveness in employees, which can lead to even more stress.

Very few people can put up with the day-to-day barrage of unhappy patrons who expect to be treated poorly.

Remember that, at the most basic level, we are all motivated to act in a particular way because our action will either

a. Result in a gain (reward).

   or

b. Avoid a loss (punishment).

Giving good customer service, even in non-profit situations, can satisfy both motivations for the giver. People who provide good customer service, regardless of the nature of their business, *earn psychological benefits* in addition to any rewards offered by their organizations.

If you are frustrated or unhappy in your job now, take an objective look at the kind of service you are giving. In almost every case, your job satisfaction mirrors the satisfaction people feel when doing business with you. Giving poor service is a way of beating up on yourself!

So regardless of the profit aims of your organization, giving good service makes sense for you as an individual. It also makes a lot of sense for you as a member of an organization. Organizational success often affects your individual success. The satisfaction of developing professionalism and doing a job competently and effectively is its own reward.

IDEA 6.
UNDERSTAND THE TERRIBLE COST OF THE LOST CUSTOMER.

Most people don't understand the real cost of a lost customer. When an unhappy customer decides to stop doing business with us, the costs are much more than we realize. We talked earlier, in Idea 3, about the fact that most unhappy customers don't complain to you, but they almost all complain *about* you. And that can cost you dearly.

To get a clearer view of the real costs, let's consider a business we can all identify with: a grocery supermarket. Here's a story of Mrs. Williams, a lady who has been shopping at Happy Jack's Supermarket[4] for many years but who has decided to stop shopping there. Although a regular customer for years, she has never felt that her business is appreciated.

As you read, try to calculate the cost of these same "ripple effects" on your company.

GOODBYE MRS. WILLIAMS

There goes Mrs. Williams. She just checked out her groceries from Happy Jack's Supermarket and she's mad as hell. She's been shopping here for years but the produce man wouldn't even consider making her a smaller package of apples. The dairy department was out of the quart-size skim milk. And then the cashier demanded two forms of identification with her check. What do they think she is, a common criminal?

But worst of all was just an overall feeling that Happy Jack's employees could care less if she shops there. She spends about

50 hard-earned dollars there every week, but to the store employees she's just another cash cow to be milked without so much as a sincere "thank you." Nobody seems to care whether she's a satisfied customer.

But today is different. Mrs. Williams just decided to try shopping elsewhere. Maybe—just maybe—there is a store where they'll appreciate her business.

What do the employees think about that?

They're not worried. Happy Jack's is a pretty big chain and doesn't really need Mrs. Williams. Besides, she can be a bit cranky at times. They'll survive without her $50 a week. Too bad she's unhappy, but a big company like this can't twist itself into contortions just to save one little old lady from going down the street to the competition.

Sure, we believe in treating customers well, but we're businesspeople. Let's look at the bottom line. After all, it can hardly be considered a major financial disaster to lose a few customers like Mrs. Williams. Or can it?

The employees at Happy Jack's need to understand some economic facts of life. Successful businesses look long term. They look at the "ripple effects" of their service, not just at the immediate profit from an individual purchase.

The shortsighted employee sees Mrs. Williams as a small customer dealing with a big company. Let's change that view: Look at the situation from another, longer term perspective.

More than the loss of one small customer

The loss of Mrs. Williams is not, of course, a $50 loss. It's much, much more. She was a $50-a-week buyer. That's $2,600 a year or $26,000 over a decade. Perhaps she would shop at Happy Jack's for a lifetime, but we'll use the more conservative 10-year figure for illustration.

But the ripple effects make it much worse. Studies show that *an upset customer tells on average 11 or 12 other people about an unhappy experience.* Some people will tell many more, but let's assume that Mrs. Williams told only 11. And let's estimate, for the sake of this example, that these 11 *tell an average of five others each.* This could be getting serious!

How many people are likely to hear the bad news about Happy Jack's? Look at the math:

Mrs. Williams	1
tells eleven others	+11
who tell five each	+55
Total who heard	67

Sure, but all 67 of these people aren't going to rebel against Happy Jacks, are they? Probably not. Let's assume that of these 67 customers or potential customers, only 25 percent decide not to shop at Happy Jack's. Twenty-five percent of 67 (rounded) is 17.

Assuming that these 17 people would also be $50-a-week shoppers, Happy Jack's stands to lose:

$44,200 a year, or $442,000 in a decade

because Mrs. Williams was upset when she left the store.

Although these numbers are starting to get alarming, they are still conservative. I am told by a food retailing executive that the typical supermarket customer actually spends about $100 a week, so losing a different customer could quickly double these figures.

Take a moment and think about how much your customer spends with you. Perhaps he or she buys every month or two or only once every few years. But in almost every case, repeat business is crucial to your success. Viewing customers as one-time buyers can and will be hazardous to your financial health.

Now factor in replacement costs

Customer service research conservatively estimates that *it costs six times as much to attract a new customer*[5] (mostly advertising and promotion costs) *than it does to keep an existing one* (where costs may include giving refunds, offering samples, and replacing merchandise). One report put these figures at about $19 to keep a customer happy versus $118 to get a new buyer into the store.

Again, some quick math shows the real cost of the lost Mrs. Williams:

Cost of keeping Mrs. Williams happy (includes throwing away the extra half head of lettuce)	$19
Cost of attracting 17 new customers	$2006

Now let's make our economic "facts of life" even more meaningful to us.

HOW THE LOST CUSTOMER CAN MEAN A LOST JOB

You can easily calculate the approximate amount of sales needed to pay employee salaries. Assuming that a company pays 50 percent in taxes and earns a profit of 5 percent after taxes, the following chart shows how much must be sold to pay each employee (in three different salary levels) and maintain current profit levels:

Salary	Benefits	After Tax Cost	Sales Needed
$25,000	$11,500	$18,250	$365,000
$15,000	$ 6,900	$10,950	$219,000
$10,000	$ 4,600	$ 7,300	$146,000

These figures will vary, of course. But the impact on one's job can be clearly shown.

If a $10,000-a-year clerk irritates as few as three or four customers *in a year*, the ripple effects can exceed the amount of sales needed to maintain that job! Unfortunately, many organizations have employees who irritate three or four customers *a day*! Ouch.

APPLYING MRS. WILLIAMS TO YOUR COMPANY

What does Mrs. Williams and the grocery store example have to do with you and your business? Basically, the same things can happen. Your unhappy customer will tell other customers or potential customers. They in turn will tell even more people.

Take a few moments and go back to the Mrs. Williams example, but this time use data from your own organization. Supposing you lose one customer and some of the other statistics hold true. Take a few moments to calculate the numbers as they apply to your organization. (See page 31.) If you work for a non-profit or government agency where the dollar sales is not a relevant measure, calculate the number of people who may be aggravated or upset with you and your organization. Think in terms of the psychological price that must be paid as you deal with frustrated, angry, upset patrons on a day-to-day basis.

THE FRONTLINE TEAM MAKES ALL THE DIFFERENCE

The customer game is ultimately won or lost on the front lines—where the customer comes in contact with employees. The frontline team *is* the company in the customer's eyes. Therefore, the frontline team must see themselves as the heroes they genuinely are. Managers must support them with the tools (training, systems) needed to serve the customer heroically. Surprisingly, all too few firms understand this. [6]

Saving a fraction of the "cost of the lost" can solidify a company's competitive position. Profits maintained can be spent improving employee work environment, giving raises, or keeping good people employed.

The best way to avoid losing customers is to provide them with positive experiences. The best experiences are those that exceed expectations in some positive ways. Surprise your customers with service that is better than they expected (or, at least, less bad than they had feared).

Calculating the Cost of Your Lost Customer

Use these guidelines to calculate the potential cost of your lost customers.

Annual Revenue lost:

1. Estimate the average or typical dollar amount spent by your customers: $_____ *per visit*

2. Calculate the annual dollar amount: $_____

3. Calculate the dollar amount spent in a decade: $_____

4. Multiply the annual dollar amount x 17 (people who may follow an unhappy customer cost the door): $_____

    Then,

5. Add customer replacement costs of 17 customers ($118 is a typical figure): (E.g. 17 × $118) $_____

    Minus the cost of keeping your present customer happy ($19 is a typical figure): (E.g. # of present customers × $19) $_____

    "Replacement" costs = $_____

    Finally,

6. Total the revenue lost figures (annual or per decade) plus replacement costs. . . a rough cost of your lost: $_____

Note: These calculations are designed only to get you thinking about the ripple effects of unhappy customers. Their mathematical precision is not guaranteed nor is it that important. The point is, lost customers cost a lot of money.

IDEA 7.
UNDERSTAND THE IMPORTANCE OF
EXCEEDING CUSTOMER EXPECTATIONS.

Exceeding expectations has become almost a cliche in customer service. While the phrase is overused, the principle is sound. We can earn customers' loyalty by exceeding their expectations in positive ways.

To understand how this process works, we need to review a few facts about what motivates people. In short, people are motivated to act in a particular way because their action will result in a gain (reward) or allow them to avoid a loss (punishment). Customers are rational people. If a buying experience is positive, they will probably come back; if negative, they'll try to avoid returning.

But that is an oversimplification. In some situations, such motivation is not quite so clear-cut. Management theorist Frederick Herzberg taught that the opposite of an unhappy worker (or customer) is not necessarily a motivated one. He taught that satisfaction and motivation are two separate factors, not two ends of the same scale. His theory caused us to rethink the relationship between satisfaction and motivation.

Applying this thinking to customer behaviors would suggests that customers who are satisfied may be *inert*, not motivated as earlier thinkers assumed. Their satisfaction simply means the *absence of dissatisfaction*, not the motivation to become a repeat customer. A "zone of indifference" lies between the dissatisfied and the motivated.

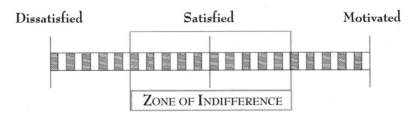

Herzberg's theory would suggest that the satisfied customer in the above model is one whose basic needs are met such that he is not suffering dissatisfaction. He is in a neutral state. The services he received were adequate.

But to *motivate* the customer to return, something more than adequate satisfaction must be experienced. The challenge, then, is to get beyond satisfaction to motivation. To do so, we must consider the crucial role of customer expectations.

As customers entering into a buying experience, we expect (perhaps unconsciously) to be treated a particular way. What we expect is often based on our past associations with the seller, the organization, or companies we see as similar. If we had a good experience with that person or company before, we'll probably expect something satisfactory. If the last transaction wasn't so positive, we might assume the next one won't be any better.

Objective and perceived expectations

These expectations are *perceptual*. They exist in the mind of our customer. Sometimes they are accurate and rational, sometimes they aren't. They reflect an overall reaction to the whole buying experience.

When we judge the quality of a tangible product, we use more objective (less perceptual) standards. For example, if we buy a new automobile we may judge its quality by things such as its:

- Workmanship (it seems to be well built, nice paint job).
- Reliability (it starts and runs well).
- Low frequency of repair (it seldom has to be fixed).
- Appropriate size (it holds my family comfortably).
- Price relative to its quality.

Likewise when we judge the quality of a service (for example, a house painter's job) we measure it by objective (less perceptual) standards such as:

- The work was done on time (he met the deadline).
- The surfaces to be painted were carefully prepared.
- The paints were mixed and applied neatly.
- The painter cleaned up after the job.

These kinds of objective standards are much the same for each customer. But evaluating customer satisfaction *with the entire experience* goes beyond the core product or service bought. It looks at how the customer's expectations were met or exceeded.

Expectations will be different among different organizations or under differing circumstances. People expect different treatment from a full-service department store than they do from a discount warehouse store. They expect different service from a prestigious law firm and a state auto license bureau. For that matter, they probably expect something different from the same store at different times: perhaps a little less personal attention during busy periods (like Christmas shoppers or end-of-month license-plate buyers).

DIFFERENT EXPECTATIONS FROM DIFFERENT BUSINESSES

If you shop at a self-service discount store, you expect to be treated in a particular way. You do not necessarily expect that the clerk (if you can find one) in the clothing department will be an expert in fitting clothing. Nor would you be likely to expect that person to be particularly helpful in choosing or color-coordinating items you may want to purchase. This is not to say that some people who work there would not have these skills, but we probably wouldn't expect them as a general rule.

If we simply select some clothing items from a rack and take them to a checkout for purchase, we are not surprised nor particularly disappointed. That's about what we expected, and if other aspects of the store are okay (it seems clean and well stocked, for instance), we could be perfectly satisfied.

By contrast, if we were to go to an exclusive boutique, we would expect a different kind of transaction. We would probably expect an employee to have considerable expertise in clothing fit, color, and materials. We might realistically expect that service person to give us individual attention and assistance as we make our purchases.

When we find situations like these just described, our expectations are met. Dissatisfaction is probably avoided; we are in that *zone of indifference*. The motivation to become a loyal customer, however, lies not in meeting expectations but in *exceeding* them.

Getting customers beyond the zone of indifference is the goal. The key to motivating a customer to feel loyalty, however, lies not in meeting what the customer anticipates but in *exceeding* it. To do this, you need to have some concept of what the customer anticipates.

How can you best anticipate changing customer needs?

STAY CLOSE TO CUSTOMERS TO CLARIFY WHAT THEY ANTICIPATE

Nothing is more important to building loyalty than staying close to your customers and maintaining an ongoing dialogue. To do so requires every company member to be a sensing device, a curious, information gatherer.

Three things are necessary for ongoing customer sensing:

1. Employees who are taught to and rewarded for getting customer feedback.

2. Processes for harvesting and using customer feedback.

3. Empowered employees who respond to customer feedback in productive ways.

What can you do with the input received from customers? You can use it to best understand what they anticipate when doing business with you. Customer perceptions are exceptionally valuable data. Only when we have a sense of what is anticipated can we exceed expectations and thus build customer loyalty. Ultimately, today's customer service success arises from a central theme that is simple to state yet challenging to implement. The underlying theme is:

> You achieve customer satisfaction, retention, and loyalty by exceeding what customers anticipate in positive ways.

THE CONCEPT OF A-PLUS[7]

I call the process of exceeding what customers anticipate *A-Plus*. Research and the experience of countless experts points to A-plus thinking as almost a "master key" to service success.

As customers compare what they anticipate with the service received, one of three situations will show up:

1. The experience was not as positive (or was more negative) than the customer anticipated.

2. The experience was pretty much what the customer anticipated.

3. The experience was more positive (or less negative) than the customer anticipated.

In the condition described in number 1, the customer's experience was not very good. She's dissatisfied and likely to defect to another provider, if she has a rational alternative.

In the condition described in number 2, the customer is neither dissatisfied nor particularly motivated to return. This person is in the zone of indifference we discussed earlier.

In the condition described in number 3, the transaction was better than anticipated. Either the customer thought it would be pretty good and it was very good, or the customer thought it would not be particularly good but it wasn't as bad as anticipated. If positive anticipations were sufficiently exceeded (or negative one's shown to be unfounded), this customer is a very good candidate for repeat business.

This number 3 situation is what I call an *A-Plus* experience: customer anticipations were *exceeded* in positive ways.

WHY A-PLUS LEADS TO CUSTOMER RETENTION

To understand how A-Plus works, we need to review a little theory. Now don't yawn. Theories need not be convoluted or hard-to-understand explanations using a lot of scientific jargon. In fact, the best theories are relatively simple to understand and provide excellent guidelines for their application. The old saying about being "okay in theory but won't work in practice" creates an artificial division. Good theory is applicable, and the theory I'm about to describe is an excellent, usable one.

"Equity theory," from the field of social psychology, provides a solid theoretical basis for predicting that the A-plus customer will become a repeat customer. Psychologist J. Stacy Adams first articulated this theory in the mid-1960s, and many others tested it throughout the 1970s and beyond. It has stood the test of time to become widely accepted as a predictor of some kinds of human behavior. Here is a quick summary of the theory:

Equity theory starts with the premise that human beings constantly go into and out of various kinds of relationships ranging from the intimate to the cursory. The buyer-seller relationship is germane to this discussion.

Once in a relationship, even a brief one, people regularly assess the *relative equity or fairness of their involvement* compared to other people. They check to see if what they give to the relationship seems appropriate to what they are getting out of it. A very simple example of a relationship that is out of balance (incquitable) would arise if you give something (a tangible gift, a greeting, or a special favor) and receive nothing in return.

Inequitable relationships feel awkward and often uncomfortable. Common courtesy dictates that he do something to "re-balance" the relationship. When invited to dinner, people strive to re-balance by bring something to share at the meal, or a hostess gift, or the like. Or, the guest invites the hostess to something. This is ingrained in social mores of most cultures. People who take but never give are soon found lonely.

Much of the early testing of inequitable relationships focused on the workplace, where worker perceptions of fairness (equity) were correlated with certain behaviors. In other words, we looked at what people do when they feel inequitably treated. Not surprisingly, studies found that people who, for example, were paid less for doing the same work as others felt a sense of inequity. In my own doctoral dissertation, I found that employees who sensed that their supervisor communicated more often and more positively with other employees in the workgroup (compared to themselves) felt a clear sense of inequity.[8]

The theory goes beyond simply citing situations where people may feel inequitably treated. It also predicts what people are likely to do about it. When inequity is perceived, people will respond with one or some combination of the following:

- *Ignore or rationalize the inequity.* (The offended person makes up a reason: "He deserves to be treated better than I do," "The world isn't fair but I'm not going to fight it," or "I guess he didn't hear me say hello.")

- *Demand restitution.* (The offended person goes to the boss to demand a fairer pay, or the customer wants her money back when product quality is poor.)

- *Retaliation.* (The offended person tells others about how bad the organization is, does harm to the person seen as the cause of the inequity, or engages in outright sabotage.)

- *Withdraw from the relationship.* (The offended person quits the relationship and doesn't come back.)

So far this theory seems to bear out common sense. If we feel we are being unfairly treated, we get upset and usually do something about it. Hence, the unsatisfied participant in a relationship (the customer in our case) is likely to do one of these things. The first two alternatives may give you as a business a chance to patch things up and retain the customer using recovery techniques such as those described elsewhere in this book. (See the Powerful Ideas bearing the 😀.) But the last two—retaliation or withdrawal—can be devastating. Mrs. Williams, the former Happy Jack's Super Market customer in Powerful Idea 6, did both. She withdrew—quit shopping there— and retaliated by telling her friends, thus starting the negative ripple effects that may have resulted in scores or even hundreds of lost customers or potential customers.

APPLYING THE POSITIVE SIDE OF EQUITY THEORY

Here is where the theory gets even more interesting: People who feel that they are receiving more than they "deserve" from a transaction also experience a psychological need to restore the balance of fairness. A simple illustration of this is the psychological pressure you may feel to reciprocate when someone does something unusually nice for you. The relationship will remain unbalanced until you re-balance it with a similar kindness or some other positive action.

Herein lies the theoretical basis for our A-plus strategy, for exceeding customer anticipations. By going beyond what people anticipate, you create an imbalance that, for many people, will require action on their part to re-balance. The logical options are the opposite of what victims of a negative imbalance feel. They could rationalize or ignore it, of course, but attempts to restore the balance could also take the form of telling others of the positive experience, paying a premium for the goods received, or, in short, becoming a loyal customer.

The challenge, then, is to *create positive imbalances by exceeding what customers anticipate.* This is the master key to creating an A-plus strategy for building customer loyalty and growing customer capital.

PUT THE A-PLUS STRATEGY TO WORK

Putting the A-plus strategy to work requires two kinds of ongoing actions:

1.   Continually work to understand what customers anticipate, and then

2.   Exceed what is anticipated ("A-plusing").

I'll be showing you many ways to exceed expectations—to A-plus customers—throughout this book. Each has the power to motivate your customer to become loyal to you and your company.

PART II

Powerful Ideas for Projecting Your Personality to Customers

The opening moments with a customer, whether face to face, over the phone, via letter or advertisement, or through a Web site, can be critical to building a foundation for loyalty. The old adage, "You only get one chance to make a first impression," is true. You can, in some cases, recover from a bad first contact, but it takes a lot of additional work. Why not get it right the first time? Be sure you are applying tips like the ones in this section.

IDEA 8.
GREET CUSTOMERS AND BUILD INSTANT RAPPORT.

Woody Allen once said that 80 percent of success is just showing up. In customer service, 80 percent of success is treating the customer like a guest who just showed up. Whether the customer comes to you in person or via a phone call or Web site hit, greet him or her warmly. For Web sites, the word *welcome* can be powerful. On the phone, a friendly, cheerful greeting does much to set a foundation for a good relationship.

When guests come to your home, you greet them, right? You say "hello" or "hi there." Yet we've all had the experience of being totally ignored by service people in some businesses. A friendly greeting is one of those little things that mean a lot.

GREET YOUR CUSTOMER PROMPTLY

A study clocked the number of seconds people had to wait to be greeted in several businesses. Researchers then asked customers how long they'd been waiting. In every case, the customer's estimate of the time elapsed was much longer than the actual time. A customer waiting 30 or 40 seconds often feels like it's been three or four minutes! Time drags when you're waiting to be noticed. With electronic commerce, people have the attention span of a gnat. If you cannot give them immediate attention, they will quickly leave.

In face-to-face interactions, a prompt greeting reduces customer stress. Why would customers feel stress? Remember, they are usually on unfamiliar turf. They are likely to feel somewhat uncomfortable. You work there every day; they are just visiting.

A quick, friendly greeting starts to relax the customer and greases the wheels of smooth service.

Some fast-food restaurants do a good job of sending out an employee to "take orders" from people standing in line.

One place I frequently go has someone greet you and write your order on a slip of paper that she hands back to you. You then give the food order to the cash register clerk when you get there. The psychological effect is that you feel that you have already ordered, and therefore probably won't look at the line ahead of you and leave. In reality, of course, you haven't ordered until the cash register clerk calls in the order, but by being greeted promptly and by giving the greeter your order, you have made a perceptual commitment to stay.

SPEAK UP!

Verbally greet a customer within 10 seconds of the time he or she comes into your store or approaches your work location. Even if you are busy with another customer or on the phone, pause to say hello and let them know that you'll be ready to help them soon.

We have all had experiences where a business lost us simply because it didn't greet us. Here's my example: A watch repairman ran a shop in my hometown. His shop was tiny and cramped, but his reputation for craftsmanship was excellent. I came to his shop and found him bent over a counter working with another customer. I squeezed in behind the customer and waited for the repairman to greet me. He didn't. After a few minutes, I felt uncomfortable—as though I were invisible. I decided to leave and "come back later," which, of course, I never did. A simple, momentary action of looking up from the customer he was working with and perhaps saying "I'll be with you in a minute" would have saved me as a customer.

Always acknowledge your customers. Promptly.

TALK TO CUSTOMERS WITH YOUR EYES

Even in situations where you may not be able to say hello out loud to an approaching customer, you can make eye contact. Simply looking at your customer tells them much about your willingness to serve. (My watch repairman mentioned previously should have done this.)

As with your greeting, your timing is important. The 10-second rule also applies here. Make eye contact with a customer within 10 seconds, even if you are busy with another person. Quicker is better.

Eye contact creates a bond between you and the customer. It conveys your interest in communicating further. It builds rapport. You don't have to interrupt what you are doing with another customer. Just a pause and a quick look "captures" new customers into an obligation to deal with you further, greatly reducing the chance they'll feel ignored and leave.

When working with customers, be sensitive to *how* you look at them. Communication expert Bert Decker says that the three "I's" of eye communication are intimacy, intimidation, and involvement. Intimacy (like when we're expressing love) and intimidation (when we want to exert power) are both communicated by looking directly at another person for a long period—from 10 seconds to a minute or more.

But most communication in business settings calls for Decker's third "I"—involvement. In our culture, people create involvement by looking at the other person for five- to 10-second periods before looking away briefly. This is generally comfortable for people. If you look away more often than that, you may be seen as "shifty" or suspicious; if you lock in eye contact for longer, it feels like intimidation or intimacy.

Eye contact is a powerful communication tool. Be sensitive to ways you use it.

SMILE

As the old adage goes, "Smile. It'll make people wonder what you've been up to." But more importantly, it'll tell customers that they came to the right place and are on friendly grounds.

Keep in mind that a smile originates in two places: the mouth and the eyes. A lips-only version looks pasted on, insincere. It's like saying "cheese" when being photographed.

It doesn't fool anyone. The eyes, however, are the windows to the soul and tell the truth about your feelings toward people.

Smile with your eyes and your mouth. Let your face show that you're glad your guest arrived. Remember, you are not dressed for work until you put on a smile.

Now, in fairness, some people smile more readily than others. For some a more serious facial expression is comfortable and natural. But in American culture, a smile is both expected and appreciated when one is meeting people. If you don't smile spontaneously, practice it. It need not be a Cheshire Cat, ear-to-ear grin (in fact that may *really* get people wondering about you) but just a pleasant, natural smile.

Look too at your eyebrows. Some people who knit their brows appear to be scowling, even when they don't intend to. Look at yourself in the mirror. Work on facial expression as an actor would.

Idea 9.
Apply good conversation skills.

The best way to start a conversation depends on what the customer needs. In many cases, especially in retail stores, customers need first to be reassured that this is a "nice friendly place" to do business. They need to dispel worries about being pressured into buying something they don't want. Use a non-threatening ice-breaker.

Often customers want to browse and get the feel of the place before they commit to doing business. The best ice-breaker for the browser can be an off-topic, friendly comment. Some good ones might be:

- A *compliment.* ("That's a very sharp tie you're wearing." or "Your children are sure cute. How old are they?")

- *Weather related.* ("Isn't this sunshine just beautiful?" or "Some snowfall, isn't it?")
- *Small talk.* (Look for cues about one's interests in sports, jobs, mutual acquaintances, past experiences, and so on.)

If a browsing customer seems to be focusing attention on a product (for example, he is holding several shirts or is looking at a particular line of products), he can be reclassified as a "focused shopper." The best ice-breaker for the focused shopper is one that is more specific to the buying decision. It may:

- *Anticipate the customer's questions* ("What size are you looking for, sir?" or "Can I help you select a _____.")
- *Provide additional information* ("Those shirts are all 25 percent off today" or "We have additional sizes in the stock room.")
- *Offer a suggestion or recommendation* ("Those stripe suits are really popular this season" or "If you need help with measurements, our estimators can figure out what you'll need.")

Be attentive to customers' needs. Give them time to browse if that's what they need, but be responsive to them in helping make a buying decision when they are ready to buy.

UNDERSTAND THE CHARACTERISTICS OF GOOD
CONVERSATIONS AND INTERVIEWS[1]

Both conversations and interviews are one-to-one communications that allow two-way sharing of information and feelings. They can be highly effective ways to gather ideas, build relationships, and solve problems. Their effectiveness depends in large part on the degree and quality of interaction between the participants. Interaction means that both parties have ample *opportunity* to participate. If one party monopolizes the conversation, both sides lose.

If your job calls for interviewing customers (to gather information or assess their needs) and you find yourself talking uninterruptedly for as long as two or three minutes, you are probably failing to maximize this communication medium. Any interview should include a good deal of give-and-take. Thus, creating an environment that is "safc" for interaction is an important task for the interviewer. This is accomplished largely by not monopolizing the conversation and by soliciting and encouraging feedback with good listening skills.

UNDERSTAND THE NATURE AND FUNCTIONS OF CONVERSATION

Conversations are one-to-one communication that is less structured than most interviews. Each culture has unique ways of conversing. When people from different cultures interact, they frequently feel ill at ease, and they often misjudge or misunderstand each other. To reduce the communication problems that arise in multicultural situations, it is helpful if you know something about the communicative styles of the majority of the people with whom you work. (We are not talking just about national cultures, but also about subcultures in which people from varying groups apply different communication styles.)

CONVERSATIONS, AMERICAN STYLE

The following are some generalizations about the communicative culture found in most American businesses.[2] These are, of course, *generalizations*:

↪ *Preferred topics.* In casual conversation (what we call "small talk"), Americans prefer to talk about the weather, sports, jobs, mutual acquaintances, and past experiences, especially ones they have in common with their conversation partners. Most Americans are taught to avoid discussing politics and religion, especially with people they do not know well, because politics and religion are considered controversial topics. Sex, bodily functions, and emotional problems are considered very personal topics and are likely to be discussed only with close friends or professionals trained to help.

By contrast, people in some other cultures are taught to believe that politics and/or religion are good conversation topics, and they may have different ideas about what topics are too personal to discuss with others.

↪ *Favorite forms of verbal interaction.* In a typical conversation between Americans, no one talks for very long at a time. Participants in conversations take turns speaking frequently, usually after the speaker has spoken only a few sentences. In addition, Americans prefer to avoid arguments. If an argument is unavoidable, they prefer it to be restrained, carried on in a normal conversational tone and volume.

Americans are generally impatient with ritual conversational exchanges that don't really convey much meaning. Nevertheless, a few expressions are common. For example, "How are you?" "Fine, thank you, how are you?" Or, "It was nice to meet you." "Same here." Or the cliche, "Have a nice day."

People from other cultures may be more accustomed to speaking and listening for longer periods when they are in conversation, or they may be accustomed to more ritual interchanges (about the health of family members, for example) than Americans are. They may enjoy argument, even vigorous argument, of a kind that Americans are likely to find unsettling.

↪ *Depth of involvement preferred.* Americans do not generally expect very much personal involvement from conversational partners. Small talk—without long silences that provoke uneasiness—is enough to keep matters going smoothly. In the workplace, Americans rarely discuss highly personal topics, which include financial matters. Many Americans are very uncomfortable if you ask how much money they make or the cost of something they own. Personal topics are reserved for conversations between very close friends or with professional counselors. However, American women tend to disclose more personal information to each other than do American men.

Some people from other cultures prefer even less personal involvement than Americans do and rely more on ritual interchanges. Others come from cultures where personal information is openly discussed.

↳ *Tone of voice and non-verbal behaviors.* Most American business people are verbally adept, have a good vocabulary, speak in moderate tones, and use some gestures of the arms and hands. Touching behaviors in normal business communication are usually limited to a handshake or occasional pat on the back.

By contrast, other cultures might be accustomed to louder voices or many people talking at once. Likewise, people from different cultures vary in such things as vigorous use of hands and arms to convey emphasis, more touching between conversation partners, and use of personal space (such as how far apart people stand or sit).

Apply basic conversation skills

Conversing with all kinds of people can be a very pleasant experience—and a valuable business skill. The following are some suggestions on how to initiate and sustain effective conversations.

↳ *Have something to talk about.* Good conversation is a process of finding topics of common interest. It stands to reason that the more topics you know something about, the more comfortable you'll be in talking with people.

↳ *Be well read.* Regularly read magazines and newspapers. Also, tune into quality broadcast programs. Good conversationalists pick up a lot of information from in-depth news shows, documentaries, and quality programming. Public radio and broadcast talk shows can also stimulate thinking and keep us up to date. Make it a point to listen to people. Note what they talk about in conversations. Some typical topics you may hear include sports, TV news or current events, magazine reports, organizational changes or news, personal or family news, gossip, entertainment, or politics.

↳ *Find your conversation partners' interests.* Think about the interests of people with whom you'd like to converse. Identify one or two topics you know that person likes to talk about. You may find, for example, that Bob is a 49'ers football fan, Robin loves sports cars, Sharon is active in a support group for women, and Lynn plays drums in a band. Then, try to learn something about the topics others are interested in. Once learned, mention this information when talking with them. Don't proclaim what you've learned as though you're a new expert, but use what you know to ask how they feel about the topic. Then be a good listener. You'll learn more and strengthen your relationship.

↳ *Practice conversation starters and sustainers.* Learn to make small talk, initiate conversations, and keep those conversations from dying. Use support listening techniques and open-ended questions such as "What do you think of the changes in the course requirements?" or "Where do you think the stock market is headed?"

↳ *Practice conversation closers.* Don't get trapped in endless discussion. Learn ways to end a conversation without being abrupt or rude. Use non-verbal cues to indicate that you need to end the conversation (look at your watch; begin to move away from your partner). Also use subtle verbal cues that you want to end the conversation ("Well, it'll be inter*esting to see the effects on class enrollment"* or *"I'll get back to you if I hear anything new"*). *Sometimes, however, being direct is better ("Oops, I better get back to my homework").*

↳ Be willing to make time for conversation. If you don't take time for some social conversation, you may send unspoken messages to others that you are aloof or not interested in them.

AVOID INAPPROPRIATE CONVERSATION

As I mentioned earlier, other than your closest friends, people don't normally want to hear about your personal problems. (One exception: your supervisor when the problem affects your work.) As a TV talk show host quipped: "Eighty percent of the people don't care, and the other 20 percent are *glad* you've got problems, too."

Complaints about your boss, co-workers, company, or school may come across as whining or inappropriate griping. Everybody has relationship problems at times. Unless you are seeking advice from a close friend or trusted advisor on how to improve the situation, keep your negative opinions to yourself. And when starting conversations with people you don't know well, avoid the more sensitive topics like politics, gossip, and topics where people may have strong or opposite feelings.

The acceptability of topics changes from time to time. For example, years ago hunting would have been a safe topic among many people. Today, with increasing concern about animal rights, hunting talk can create serious controversy. By contrast, some subjects once considered very personal are now more openly discussed. So stay in tune with current issues and controversies.

➥ As a general rule, *avoid*

- Criticizing or belittling others.
- Griping about the company, department, or classroom.
- Passing on gossip or hurtful comments about others.
- Using excessive profanity.
- Stirring up bad feelings among people.
- Making racial, religious, or gender insults.
- Flirting or using comments with unwanted sexual overtones.

➥ As a general rule, *do*

- Make your comments positive and upbeat.
- Be supportive of other people.
- Give others the benefit of the doubt.
- Compliment freely and often.
- Acknowledge peoples' accomplishments, birthdays, and religious holidays—respectfully.

IDEA 10.
GET THE CUSTOMER EXPERIENCING SOMETHING.

Telling people about your products or services isn't usually enough. Showing them how it works is much better. But to really serve your customers, get them involved—get their hands on your products in some way and they'll feel better about you and your company.

Studies of successful computer salespeople, for example, show that they encourage customers to sit down at the computer as soon as possible to get them playing with it. They don't dazzle (or confuse) the customer with hi-tech jargon or even information about the machine's capabilities. They get them *doing something*. Likewise, the best auto salespeople invite customers to sit in and test drive the car right away.

Other, less obvious ways to get people doing something:

- Personally hand them a shopping cart, basket, or sales literature.

- Ask them to begin filling out paperwork.

- Get them to touch the product.

- Offer a beverage, a piece of candy, cookies, or fruit, while they wait.

- Offer a product flyer, information packet, video presentation, or sample to review.

It doesn't matter so much *what* they do, so long as they begin to do *something*. Involvement leads to commitment. The more time and effort customers invest in a relationship with you, the more likely they will stick with it.

"TRY SOME RETAILTAINMENT"

Wal-Mart's annual report describes their attempts at blending retailing with entertainment to "create a fun, dynamic shopping environment." The goal is to add excitement to the shopping experience and make the store a good place for customers and associates (employees) alike. "Every store is encouraged to create its own 'wild and crazy' retailtainment events specifically designed for its individual community. Local stores invite clubs and civic organizations to set up exhibits, or ask police and fire departments to conduct safety seminars and demonstrations. To raise money for local charities last year, stores engaged in everything from a ladder drive (in which associates volunteered to sit on top of a ladder until they solicited a certain amount in donations) to Bingo for Seniors, which raised money for the Children's Miracle Network."[3]

The company also uses free concerts (live local bands or closed circuit live broadcasts of super stars like Ricky Martin and Faith Hill), and virtually hundreds of other ideas to make shopping at Wal-Mart and experience not just a chore.

What could you do to make your customers' experiences more entertaining and memorable? How else can you exceed what is anticipated and move the customer from the zone of indifference toward motivation to return?

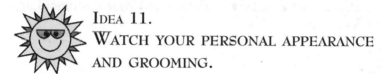

IDEA 11.
WATCH YOUR PERSONAL APPEARANCE AND GROOMING.

From the moment we meet people, we begin to size them up. We begin to draw conclusions about them almost immediately. What we decide about their trustworthiness and ability is largely a factor of first impressions. And, as the old saying goes, you only get one chance to make that first impression.

The key word in dress and grooming is *appropriate*. If in doubt about what is appropriate dress and grooming, look at what other *successful* people are doing. You need not be a copycat or wear an outfit you hate, but do consider what other role models do. And then meet or exceed their appearance.

An owner of an auto repair shop tried an experiment. Each of his repair people was paid on commission for the amount of repair work he or she did. He invited the mechanics to volunteer to change their dress and grooming. Several agreed to cut their hair shorter, shave daily, and wear clean uniforms.

The outcome: Those who did created far more repeat business than the others. The customers would ask for the better dressed mechanics and those who chose to dress and groom themselves in the "old way" found themselves getting less work.

Remember, the key word in dress and grooming is appropriate. Salespeople in a surf shop would look foolish in three-piece suits; an undertaker would look ludicrous in a Hawaiian sport shirt. To overcome problems of individual differences that may be ineffective, some organizations issue uniforms. These may be coveralls, full uniforms, or partial uniforms such as blazers, vests, name badges, or work shirts. Some employees like these (they save on the costs of a wardrobe), while some resist the sameness of the uniformed look.

Determine what level of professionalism you want to convey to your customers, then create a look that projects your competence. Pay attention to details and your customers notice these things.

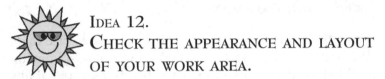

Idea 12.
Check the appearance and layout of your work area.

"A cluttered desk is the sign of a cluttered mind," reads the desk plaque. Likewise, a cluttered work area conveys a sense of disorganization and low professionalism.

Look around you and see what your customer sees. Is merchandise displayed attractively? Is the place clean and tidy? Does the workspace look like an organized, efficient place?

Check for barriers

Often people arrange their workspace with a desk, counter, or table between them and the customer. While sometimes this is necessary, often it creates a barrier—both physical and psychological—between the customer and the one serving. Try inviting customers to sit beside your desk with you instead of across from you. Try using a small round table, especially when customers need to read materials you give them. Some auto dealerships have removed all sales office desks and replaced them with small round tables. Now the customer and salesperson sit around the table and work together to make a deal. You don't feel like you are on opposite sides, in "combat" with each other, when the table is round.

CONSIDER CUSTOMER COMFORT

Are your customers invited to sit in a comfortable chair? Does your office or store invite them to relax? Are waiting areas furnished with reading materials, perhaps a TV? Are vending machines available? Is the vending area kept clean?

A small auto body shop I visited surprised me. It had a waiting room that looked like a living room in a nice home. Easy chairs, a TV, coffee table with recent magazines, even fresh flowers. Take a look at your work areas from the customer's viewpoint.

 IDEA 13.
USE GOOD TELEPHONE TECHNIQUES.

Often your only contact with customers is via the phone. Make the most of it.

The telephone certainly can be, as the ads used to say, "The next best thing to being there." Despite expanded use of e-mail, Internet, and electronic communications, few experts foresee the demise of what old-time Bell Telephone employees used to call POTS: plain old telephone service. No one has yet found a substitute for one-to-one, person-to-person, real-time voice communications. In fact, no business can long survive without a phone. At some point customers will want to talk with you, not just a machine. These experiences can become defining moments in your relationship. Done well, excellent telephone techniques can provide great service and build rapport with your callers.

Too often, however, a phone conversation becomes a customer turnoff rather that a relationship builder. Ill-informed or poorly trained employees can cost companies tremendously in lost goodwill and lost customers. The costs do not stop with the caller who is poorly handled. Ripple effects can run deep when an organization gets a reputation for poor phone call handling. Some large organizations or government agencies, for example, have earned horrible reputations among callers who cannot get through busy lines, or who face impolite or inefficient call handling, inaccurate or conflicting information, and the inability to get through the automatic switching to a live human being.

Customers often want to talk to real people, except for routine transactions that can be done by inputting numbers. Some common transactions that can avoid live-person help are checking balances at a financial institution or on a credit card, checking flight arrival times, changing investment options in a retirement plan, or arranging newspaper delivery stop and start dates. These can be done by inputting electronic impulses to a touch-tone phone. But even for routine transactions that most people feel comfortable with, you should offer the option of speaking live to a customer service person at any time.

The root causes of poor telephone use can quickly cancel out the potential benefits of "the next best thing to being there."

Two blanket problems can be found at the root of poor phone service:

1. *Many people have never learned the basics of telephone courtesy and effectiveness.* They have been using the phone since childhood, yet they have never modified or polished phone use habits for appropriate business use. What may pass for okay, casual telephone usage at home is often totally inappropriate for business. The results can be loss of caller goodwill, customer dissatisfaction, and a severe loss of organizational image and effectiveness.

2. *Many people fail to account for the fact that callers cannot see the person they are talking with.* Video images will perhaps one day be commonplace, but for now a serious limitation of telephone use is that, without a visual component, the phone does not permit most nonverbal communication. Without visual cues to reinforce or clarify a message, the listener on the other end of the line may be easily confused or may create inaccurate impressions based on incomplete information.

Phrased another way, each telephone call creates interactions where people are operating blind—without the visual feedback that helps assign meaning to face-to-face messages. To compensate for this lack of vision, callers "fill in the blanks" to create conclusions from what they hear alone. They imagine things about the person with whom they speak and about the organization. What they hear (or do not hear) conveys subtle messages through timing, tone of voice, word choice, and interruptions. For many people, this ambiguity makes telephone use uncomfortable and even threatening. Although it is a great piece of basic technology we use every day, the telephone can also be frustrating.

A key to successful phone use is to simply *remember that your customer cannot see you.* Your challenge is to make up for all that lost nonverbal communication by using your voice effectively. The best ways to use the phone effectively:

- *Give the caller your name.* Let the caller know who you are just as you would in a face-to-face situation (where you may have a name tag or desk plaque).

- *Smile into the phone.* Somehow people can hear a smile over the phone! Some telephone pros place a mirror in front of them while they're on the phone.

- *Keep your caller informed.* If you need to look up information, tell the customer what you are doing. Don't leave them holding a dead phone with no clue as to whether you are still with them.

- *Invite the caller to get to the point.* Use questions such as "How can I assist you today?" or "What can I do for you?"

- *Commit to requests of the caller.* Tell the caller specifically what you will do and when you will get back to them. ("I'll check on this billing problem and get back to you by five this afternoon, okay?")

- *Thank the caller.* This lets the caller know when the conversation is over.

- *Let your voice fluctuate in tone, rate, and loudness.* You hold people's attention by putting a little life into your voice. Express honest reactions in expressive ways. Let your voice tones be natural and friendly.

- *Use hold carefully.* People hate being put on hold. When it's necessary, explain why and break in periodically to let them know they haven't been forgotten. If what you're doing will take longer than a few minutes, ask the caller if you can call them back. Write down your commitment to call back and don't miss it.

- *Use friendly, tactful words.* Never accuse the customer of anything; never convey that their request is an imposition.

To monitor the phone use in your organization, do some structured observations using a form like the checklist on page 61. You may want to modify this form to address specific

Telephone Use Check Sheet

Employee name: _____ Date: _____
(or department)

1. Was the phone answered after two rings or less? Yes No

2. Did the employee use an appropriate greeting? Yes No

3. Did the employee identify himself or herself
   by name?   Yes No

4. Was the employee's tone of voice pleasant and
   businesslike?   Yes No ?

5. Was the called handled efficiently without
   being abrupt?   Yes No ?

6. Did the employee provide accurate information
   or refer thecaller to an appropriate person? Yes No ?

7. Did the employee reflect the best image for
   the company?   Yes No ?

Score 2 points for every YES answer, 1 point for a ? (indicating
that you are not sure of the answer or could not fairly assess the
call), and 0 points for a NO answer.

Total Score:_____

[Add other items to customize this form for a particular
organization.]

For each "no" answer, briefly identify the inappropriate behaviors
or incorrect information. Add comments as needed:

Comments:

Average the scores for all observations by adding the total
scores and dividing by the number of observations. Compare
these results with previous surveys and track your progress.

standards or requirements of your company. Schedule a random sample of observations every month and then track your scores. Share the results with all personnel who use the phones and ask for their suggestions on ways to improve.

For more in-depth ideas on effective phone use, see my Career Press book, *Winning Telephone Tips* (to order call, 1-800-CAREER-1) or my 30-minute videotape training program with the same title produced by JWA Video in Chicago. For information, call 312-829-5100 or go online to *www.JWAVideo.com*.

IDEA 14.
SAY PLEASE AND THANK YOU.

At the risk of sounding like one of those books about "things I learned in kindergarten," *be polite*. It may seem old-fashioned and some customers won't be as polite to you, but that's not *their* job.

Okay, so this is not exactly brain surgery, but it is important. Sometimes the simplest things can make huge differences in customer perceptions, and this is an area where that is the case. Customers want to be appreciated and treating them politely conveys appreciation. I would personally fire any employee who fails to express thanks to my customers. I feel that strongly about this.

In a recent "Dear Abby" column the writer complained about salespeople who said "there you go" to conclude a transaction. That kind of comment is not an appropriate substitute for thanking the customer. Don't allow yourself or your people to slip into the bad habit of saying anything short of "thank you" or "thank you for your business."

As a closing comment in any transaction, "thank you for your business" is powerful and will be remembered. Indeed, recent research shows that the last part of a business transaction may be the most important for building loyalty.[4] What better way to conclude a transaction than with a thank you.

Please and *thank you* are powerful words for building customer rapport and creating customer loyalty. They are easy to say and well worth the effort.

IDEA 15.
ENJOY PEOPLE AND THEIR DIVERSITY.

J. D. Salinger said, "I am a kind of paranoid in reverse. I suspect people of plotting to make me happy." I'd like all of my employees to be paranoids in reverse. With an attitude like that we'd look forward to every meeting with every customer.

Of course, we quickly learn that some customers do not seem to be plotting to make us happy. Most are very pleasant. Some are unusual. A few are downright difficult.

Every person is different; each has a unique personality. But the kind of people who tend to bug us the most are the ones who are *not like us.* Recognize this. Then accept this diversity and learn to enjoy it. Know that people's needs are basically the same at some level and that treating them like guests, with dignity and courtesy, will create the most goodwill, most of the time.

WORK ON YOUR VERBAL DISCIPLINE

We all talk to ourselves regularly, and much of what we say may be judgmental. Train your self-talk and your comments to others to focus on the positive and avoid being judgmental. Instead of saying, "Can you believe that ugly dress on that lady?" say, "She dresses interestingly." Instead of saying, "This guy will nickel and dime me to death," say "This customer is very cost conscious." Instead of commenting on how overweight a person is, say, well, nothing.

ASSUME THE BEST FROM PEOPLE

We tend to get what we expect. If you anticipate an unpleasant interaction, you increase the likelihood that you will have one. So when customers come to you, expect the best from them, even if they look strange, behave unusually, or exhibit personality quirks. Be especially alert to the natural, but unproductive, tendency to be leery of people who are different from you.

At times you'll have to force yourself to avoid the negative and judgmental, but accept the challenge and you can make a game out of it.

Here is a challenge: Sincerely try for one full day to *avoid saying **anything** negative or judgmental* about another person. If you make it through the day, shoot for another day.

Verbal discipline can become a habit that pays off. You'll find yourself enjoying people more.

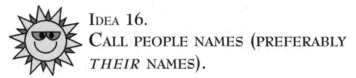

IDEA 16.
CALL PEOPLE NAMES (PREFERABLY *THEIR* NAMES).

Our name is one of our favorite sounds. Think about times when someone unexpectedly addressed you by name. Didn't it feel good? Didn't you feel less like a number and more like someone who is valued?

I had an interesting experience as the recipient of name-calling. Some 20 years ago, I moved to a new city and opened a bank account. For some reason the teller remembered my name and, the next time I went into the branch, she greeted me—by name—when I walked in the door! I was so surprised (and pleased) I became a loyal customer. I felt like I was doing business with friends.

We appreciate it when people make the effort to find out and use our name in addressing us. Here are some ways to make the most of name-calling:

- When appropriate, introduce yourself to the customer and ask his or her name.

- If you can't introduce yourself (such as when you are waiting on a line of customers), get the customer's name from their check, credit card, order form, or other paperwork.

- Avoid being overly familiar too quickly. You are normally safe calling people Mr. Smith or Ms. Jones but may be seen as rude if you call them Homer and Marge. (This is especially true when younger employees are dealing with older customers.) Better to err on the side of being too formal. If people prefer first-name address, they'll tell you so.

- If you are unsure of how to pronounce a name, ask the customer.

- If a person has an unusual or interesting name, comment on it in a positive way. (Tell a person that they have a pretty or interesting name and most will appreciate it.)

- If a person shares a name with someone in your family or a friend, comment on that.

- Try to remember the names of repeat customers. If you've forgotten one, ask a co-worker if he or she remembers. Someone usually will and you will make real points with your customer by addressing them by name.

People are usually proud of their names and will feel honored when you acknowledge it. Take the time to get and use customer names.

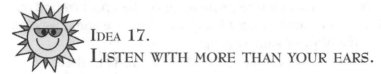

IDEA 17.
LISTEN WITH MORE THAN YOUR EARS.

Good listeners are never unpopular. It seems that all people become more interesting when they stop talking.

Pay attention to your talk-listen ratio. Avoid being so eager to tell that you forget to ask. Are you giving the customer at least equal time?

Most of us are not good listeners. We listen at about 25 percent of our potential, which means we ignore, forget, distort, or misunderstand 75 percent of what we hear. Hard to believe, perhaps, but true. Such lazy listening habits can be very costly, both to our business and to ourselves. Here are some tips for better listening:

1. *Resist distractions.* This point emphasizes the importance of concentration. Force yourself to keep your mind on what is being said.

2. *Be an opportunist.* Do your best to find areas of interest between you and your customer. Ask yourself "What's in it for me? What can I get out of what is being said? How can this information help build a relationship with this customer?"

3. *Stay alert.* It is easy to daydream if the speaker is a bit boring or if he's talking very slowly. Your thoughts may be likely to run ahead of the customer. Avoid that and instead use the extra time to evaluate, anticipate, and review. *Resist distractions.* Make the customer the center of your attention.

4. *Listen for central themes, rather than isolated facts.* Too often people get hopelessly lost as listeners because they focus in on unimportant fact and details *and miss the speaker's main point.* Judge the

content of what people are saying, not the way they are saying it. Customers may not have the "right" words, but they know what they need better than anyone.

5. *Listen as though you had to report the content* of a message to someone within eight hours. This forces you to concentrate and to remember. It is a good practice technique.

6. *Develop note-taking skills.* The simple process of writing down key points as you hear them helps you retain what you hear, even if you do not read the notes later.

7. *Hold your fire.* Don't jump to make judgments before your customer has finished talking.

8. *Work at listening.* Maintain eye contact and discipline yourself to listen to what is being said. Tune out those thoughts that get you thinking about something else.

9. *Seek clarification* from customers so you fully understand their needs. Do this in a non-threatening way using sincere, open-ended questions.

IDEA 18.
ANTICIPATE CUSTOMER NEEDS.

Margaret, a middle-aged woman, was hired to work in a local department store during the Christmas season. During a particularly hectic day, a young, pregnant mother with two toddlers holding onto her approached Margaret's cash register. Spotting the woman, Margaret excused herself from the other customers for a moment and took a chair from behind the counter to the young woman.

"Why don't you sit down here," she asked, "and I'll ring up your purchases in a few minutes and bring them back to you." The shopper was astounded and appreciative!

All Margaret had done was *anticipate customer needs* and then do something about them. She won a loyal customer for that store through her initiative and good sense. (Incidentally, the above illustration speaks well for hiring middle-aged women, especially women who have withstood the demands of raising a family. They tend to be empathetic and creative.)

Other ways we might anticipate and meet needs:

- Be sure the customer has everything needed to use the product. (If he buys paint, for example, ask if he has enough brushes, thinner, sandpaper, etc.)

- Offer to carry merchandise to the customer's car.

- Respond to the customer's urgency. If she's in a hurry, work quickly to accommodate.

- Help reduce confusion. If an application form is difficult, show your customer which parts he needs to complete and you fill in the rest.

- Be sure your customer has enough information to use the product or service. (If written directions or clarification would be useful, write some and provide photocopies to customers.)

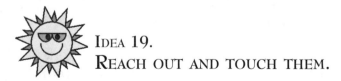 IDEA 19.
REACH OUT AND TOUCH THEM.

Physical touch is a powerful form of communication. Done appropriately, and consistent with your culture's expectations, people will feel a stronger sense of rapport with you almost immediately. At least take an opportunity to shake hands with a customer or even pat him on the back, if appropriate.

Touching is a powerful form of nonverbal communication. It can be particularly powerful when used at the end of a transaction. That's one reason that preachers greet their congregation at the end of Sunday services. It provides a positive and personal end to the interaction.

And it seems to relate to customer satisfaction in other contexts. A study of bank tellers shows the power of touch. Tellers were taught to place change in the hand of the customer rather than place it on the counter. Researchers found that customer perceptions of the bank rose sharply among customers who had been touched.

In similar studies, restaurant servers who touched their customers when serving food, giving change or a receipt, or when thanking customers found the tips they received were significantly higher.

Shaking hands is perhaps the most common form of touch in the business world. Avoid the cold fish, mechanical, or overly boisterous handshake. To add sincerity to a handshake, use the "Dolly Madison" approach: Place your left hand over their right when gripping in a handshake. But don't hold on too long.

IDEA 20.
COMPLIMENT FREELY AND SINCERELY.

Many people are hesitant about complementing others. Perhaps they think they'll sound flirtatious or condescending. But the reality is that people enjoy being complemented; we all like to be admired or appreciated.

People who compliment others are well liked. Think about your friends or acquaintances. Don't you like the ones who say nice things about you?

Complementing takes only a second and can add enormous goodwill. If you don't do this very often, get into the habit of saying something complimentary to each of your customers.

Safe ground for sincere compliments:

- *Some article of clothing they are wearing.* ("I like that tie!" "That's a beautiful sweater you have on." "That jacket looks great on you.")

- *Their children.* ("Your little boy is really cute." "How old is your daughter?" "She's a bright one." "Your son seems really sharp about computers.")

- *Their behavior.* ("Thanks for explaining exactly what you need." "I noticed you checking the_____. You're a careful shopper." "I appreciate your patience while I look this up.")

- *Something they own.* ("I like your car. What year is it?" "I noticed your championship ring. Was that last year's team?"

- *Their helpfulness.* ("Thanks for filling out that form so carefully. That'll help." "I appreciate your putting those clothes back on the rack. That makes my job easier.")

If this kind of complementing behavior seems uncomfortable to you, try to push yourself out of your comfort zone. Try this: Set a goal to give 10 sincere compliments each day. Make it a habit. Then observe the results. I'm pretty sure you will see that people like it and your popularity will increase. People love to be complemented.

PART III

POWERFUL IDEAS
FOR SOLIDIFYING REPEAT
CUSTOMERS

Relationships, whether with friends, family, or customers, don't just stay the same. They require some work, and some give and take on the part of both parties to strengthen and grow. The following tips can help solidify an ongoing relationship and build customer loyalty.

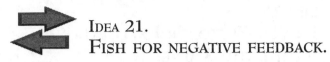

IDEA 21.
FISH FOR NEGATIVE FEEDBACK.

What?! Fish for *negative* feedback??
Exactly. Negative feedback is the kind that helps us improve. Complaining customers can be your best friends. Without their expressing problems, we could never know how to do things better for them. Without improvement, our business would stagnate and eventually fail. In customer service there is no neutral gear; we either improve or slip backward.

The best ways to get feedback is to:

- Let customers know that you really *want their honest opinions* (good news or bad).

- Provide ways for them to tell you.

USE "NAÏVE LISTENING" AND OPEN QUESTIONS

We can get such feedback in several ways, but the simplest is *naive listening*. This uses open-ended questions to let people express their ideas. An open-ended question is one that cannot be answered with a simple yes, no, or one-word response. Below are some common questions you hear everyday in businesses that can be easily changed to open-ended:

Instead of	Ask
How was everything?	*What else can I do for you?*
Can I get you something else?	*What else can I get for you?*
Did you find everything you need?	*What else can I help you find?*
Will that be all?	*What else can I do for you?*
Was everything satisfactory?	*What else could we do to better serve you?*
Did we meet your needs?	*How else can we be of help?*

Idea 22.
Exceed Customer Expectations With Extra Value.

When I ask people in my training seminars to describe value that exceeded their expectations, I hear tales of exceptional products like 15-year-old Kirby vacuum cleaners and 20-year-old Western Auto freezers. Often people talk about their Ford or Toyota pickup truck with 300,000 miles on it, a sweater that dates back a quarter century, or a consistently quick and accurate tax preparation service. Everyone seems to have a product or service that lasted longer or worked better than they would have expected.

Value is the quality of a product relative to its cost. If a product performs better, lasts longer, or costs less than expected, customer become raving fans.

Unfortunately, we don't usually have the luxury of waiting 15 or 20 years for our customers to realize our value. But there are ways to create the *perception* of value more quickly. Here are some ideas:

↪ *Packaging.* Make your product's packaging look attractive. If you sell an intangible or a service, consider ways to "package" it with some tangible reminder. For example, an insurance salesman friend of mine gave me my policies in a leather zipper binder engraved with my name on it. Gift wrapping adds to perceived value as does personalizing an item. For example, a book given as a gift is more valued if the giver (or the author) has signed it.

↪ *Guarantees or warranties.* Stand behind your products or services. Offer long-term or lifetime guarantees if possible. In most cases, a "lifetime" guarantee will result in no more product returns than a 30- or 60-day guarantee. But the perceived value is much greater.

↪ *Good product fit.* Be certain the customer is really getting the best product or service for his or her needs. Personalize and customize to the customer. One size rarely fits all. Consider using Customer Relationship Management (CRM) software to maintain customer profiles and to assure that what they buy from you really is in their best interest.

↪ *Provide experiences.* The number one Husqvarna Viking sewing machine dealer has consciously created a place where people interested in sewing come to socialize, to learn, to advise—and by the way, to buy. That's how Joe Fulmer built his Stitching Post business into a thriving $11 million business with nearly double-digit profitability. He built a community of customers through classes and other activities and that enhanced his customers' sense of value.[1]

Often, we also build customer loyalty by *reminding* them of the value they are receiving. For example:

- A city government mails information about how tax dollars are being used in the community to show its value.

- Some discount stores and supermarkets program their cash registers to show the list prices of products bought along side their discount prices and telling the customer how much she "saved."

- A manufacturer highlights its unconditional warranty in simple terms the customer can understand: "If this tool ever breaks, we will replace it free."

- An accountant clearly states that she will represent the client in any tax disputes.

Value brings customers reassurance and comfort. When we exceed customer expectations regarding value received, we create some obligation of loyalty.

Of course, another way to surprise customers with a perception of value is to give them good prices. Price is rarely the number one factor in determining value, but it is still important to most customers. Auto dealers faced with sticker-shocked customers have learned to express prices in terms of monthly payments or lease rates, not the full price. A repair shop tells customers the job will cost "about $50" and then comes in at $47.50. Customers are astonished. It actually cost *less* than expected! (Note if the price comes in at $55, you've lost the opportunity to exceed their expectations. The amount isn't as important as the fact that it went over the estimate.)

Give some thought to ways your organization exceeds pricing expectations.

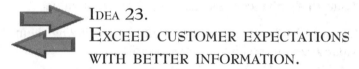

IDEA 23.
EXCEED CUSTOMER EXPECTATIONS
WITH BETTER INFORMATION.

Every product or service has an informational component. Many products include instructions for their use. Intangible goods are often accompanied by written materials that inform customers how to use them. Even a can of soup will include nutritional information and recipes. These informational aspects provide an opportunity to exceed customer expectations. Think about ways to exceed customer expectations by providing more useful, easier-to-understand information.

EXPLAIN THINGS CLEARLY

An automobile sales rep surprised me when I bought my last car. He took about 45 minutes to show me all the features of the car and how to work every one of them. He even programmed my radio to my favorite stations. It was like going through the owner's manual page by page, but much easier and more pleasant.

Solidify your customers by ensuring that they will have no problems with the products they bought. Take a moment to explain how things work and what to look out for in using them. Create clear expectations about what the product can deliver. If your product is a service, show customers how to maintain the results or continue getting benefits from it. If they will receive something in the mail, tell them when. If a followup action is necessary, explain how this will be arranged. For example:

- Following knee surgery, a teenager was assigned a physical therapist. The youth's parents expected the therapist to tell him what exercises to do and let it go at that. But the therapist exceeded expectations with some little things: She provided photocopied illustrations showing exactly how to do the exercises, she demonstrated each workout, and she called a few days later to see how he was doing.

- Whereas many car salespeople simply tell customers to look at the owner's manual in the glove box, smart sales reps spent considerable time with customers after the sale explaining all the bells and whistles on the new car. The same holds with appliance or electronics dealers. Most people like some instruction in addition to printed materials.

- A hospital changed the hallway signs when it found that guests were getting lost. They also installed color stripes on the corridor floors to direct people to various departments.

- A cellular phone dealer calls customers to see if they understand how to use all the features and offers to meet to explain them in person.

- A rental car agency offers multilingual rental agreements printed in both English and the customer's language of choice.

- A piece of office furniture that requires assembly comes with clear, well-illustrated instructions and each part clearly labeled.

USE DIFFERENT MEDIA

We can often exceed the customer's information expectations by using *different media* for product information. For example:

- Computer software includes a learning CD, videotape program, or online support.

- Some exercise equipment manufacturers include videos to teach customers how to get the most from the equipment.

- Craft shops, scrapbook supply stores, and sewing machine dealers include classes.

- Kitchenware dealers offer live cooking classes.

- Photo shops offer online photography courses.

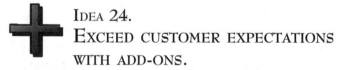

IDEA 24.
EXCEED CUSTOMER EXPECTATIONS
WITH ADD-ONS.

What add-on product or service can you give (or sell) your customers? "Freebies" are nice, but people will also appreciate appropriate add-on sales. For example, if you are buying materials for a home repair project, you will probably appreciate a store clerk who asks if you have all the needed tools or supplies.

When a shoe store clerk gives a shoehorn with a pair of new shoes or asks if you'd like to try padded inserts, he is using this opportunity area to exceed expectations. The best kinds of free add-ons are those with perceived value that exceeds their real cost. For example, the free car wash that gas stations give away with a fill-up costs them only a few cents, but its perceived value is $3 to $5. Likewise, free popcorn or drinks given away with video rentals cost 5¢ or 10¢ but have a much higher perceived value. (Have you seen the price of these in theaters lately?!) For example:

- A clerk at a supermarket hands customers a few chocolate candies with the receipt, an unexpected thank-you.

- A paint store salesperson checks to be sure that buyers have caulking, sandpaper, brushes, and a drop cloth. (These things are sold, not given away, to the appreciative customer who may have forgotten.)

- A motel staff brings out the fresh-baked chocolate chip cookies every afternoon at 4 o'clock. (The smell wafts throughout the lobby.)

- The employer brings in unexpected doughnuts for staff (internal customers) on Friday morning.

Think about small, tangible items you can give away to your customers. This opportunity area ties in closely with its marketing counterpart, add-on sales. Marketers have long recognized the value of selling current customers something else so long as they are here. This can backfire if it's too pushy, but most customers will not resent low-key inquiries about other products.

 IDEA 25.
LOOK FOR WAYS TO IMPROVE TIMING
AND FOLLOW-UP.

Nothing impresses so significantly as immediate follow-through. Successful salespeople follow up with customers (usually by phone) to see that their purchases are satisfactory. Some salespeople do this occasionally when they have a little spare time; the more successful do it regularly at scheduled times. Similarly, the best customer-oriented people (outside of sales) make commitments to customers and *always follow up*.

A simple form can help you follow up with customers and avoid commitments from dropping through the cracks. Make up your form in a notebook or on separate sheets. Include these four columns:

CUSTOMER FOLLOW-UP FORM			
Date	**Commitment** (customer name, phone, and what you promised)	**Time Due**	**Time Done**

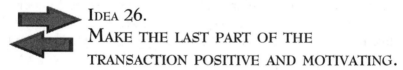

IDEA 26.
MAKE THE LAST PART OF THE
TRANSACTION POSITIVE AND MOTIVATING.

Recent studies of customer service using behavioral science principles conclude that the last moments of a service encounter are especially important in creating customer loyalty. Many people believe that both the first impressions and the last contact are equally important. Not so, say the behaviorists. The end is far more important because it is what remains in the customer's recollections. In fact, even if the opening moments weren't so good, you can make up for it with a boffo ending.

People have an innate desire for improvement. We like it when things get better and better. This desire for improvement applies to short-term encounters as well as longer relationships (and, of course, wine and cheeses, too). Even in today's technology-mediated encounters such as Web site visits, we want to see a positive progression.

In a recent *Harvard Business Review* article[2], the authors write: "[T]oo many Web encounters start strong and go downhill fast. Most companies spare no expense to make their home page attractive; a great deal of thought go into questions of aesthetics, content, and navigation in the top page or two. This is an eminently logical strategy, given the need to get people to enter and engage with a site...[but] too many Web encounters start strong and go downhill fast.... An alarming number of problems: difficulties in exiting the site if an item is out of stock, difficulty in canceling an order if the shipping charges are too high; no notification of security for credit card information, and so on. [T]he frustrated customer remembers the messy final experience far more clearly than the jazzy, supposedly sticky home page." [3]

So put special emphasis on the closing moments of a transaction and let the positive experience linger in the customer's mind.

 IDEA 27.
REASSURE THE CUSTOMER'S DECISION
TO DO BUSINESS WITH YOU.

Buyer's remorse can set in pretty fast, especially when people make an expensive purchase. At the time of sale, you can inoculate against remorse by reassuring the customer that they've made a good purchasing decision.

Phrases such as, "I'm sure you'll get many hours of enjoyment out of this" or "Your family will really love it," can help reassure and strengthen the buyer's resolve to follow through with the purchase and, as importantly, feel good about it.

A government agency might say, "I'll bet you're glad that's over with for another year," or "I'll handle the renewal—you've done all that is necessary."

A powerful tool for reassuring and expressing appreciation is the phone. One consulting approach for bank executives shows how important customer calls can be. As part of a training session, the executives develop a simple script and immediately go to the phones to call some of their customers. The conversation goes something like this:

"Hello, I'm Chris Wilson from Major Bank. I just wanted to call to let you know that we appreciate your business. You are a valued customer and we would be interested in any suggestions you might have for additional ways we could serve you."

That's about it. Let your appreciative comments sink in and then let the customer talk. The results: Customers are astounded that their banker would actually call and that he or she wasn't trying to sell anything! The image of the bank's service goes up sharply.

Contact your customers after the sale to be certain they are satisfied and getting the most value from their purchases.

IDEA 28.

MAKE SERVICE SPEED AND CUSTOMER CONVENIENCE PRIORITIES.

Constantly look for ways you can give customers quicker, easier, more convenient service than they expect. Here is an offbeat example of giving convenience:

Wal-Mart stores in some parts of the country allow owners of recreational vehicles to park their RVs overnight in the stores' lots, letting them save the cost of campground fees. A survey by the editors of a Web site called *freecampgrounds.com* found that about a third of the 227 respondents had stayed at least one night at a Wal-Mart. Says business writer Micheal Janofsky: "Music to Wal-Mart's ears; for several years now the stores have been welcoming travelers to their spacious parking lots, bringing a new definition to 'stop and shop.' While they provided none of the electrical and cable television hookups available at most campgrounds, the stores do offer the convenience of one-stop shopping for food and supplies." [4]

A recent article in *Inc.* magazine illustrates another aspect of convenience. The story quotes Thomas G. Stemberg, the founder of Staples, Inc., describing his biggest mistake. He says the biggest mistake his company made was when it decided in the mid-1980s to not enter the delivery business. "We thought we should make [the customer] come into the store and buy." His competitors delivered office products to offices everywhere. Stemberg concludes: "About two years later than our competitors, we also began to deliver. Probably over time that mistake cost us $100 million in sales and $10 million in profits." [5]

People value anything that saves them time and effort. Even services such as valet parking are growing in popularity. A recent *Wall Street Journal* piece sites a surge in valet parking for casual restaurants, shopping malls, and even hospitals. Some parking services offer car washing while customers shop. [6] You can build customer loyalty by making it easy to do business with you.

You can also build customer loyalty by surprising your customers with fast, efficient service. Federal Express has been incredibly successful by setting expectations for fast service and then beating them. They claim they'll deliver your package by 10 o'clock the next morning, but often deliver it by 9 or 9:30. A Xerox office where I once worked did something similar. We made it a point to have a repairperson arrive 15 or 20 minutes earlier than promised. In a world where business people routinely miss their appointment times, this made a huge impression.

What can you do to make speed and convenience a priority? Here are some ideas:

- *Provide it faster by having sufficient staff available.* A retailer that opens additional checkout lines when customers start backing up is being sensitive to speed and convenience.

- *Offer to deliver a product or provide on-site service.* Home and office delivery is becoming standard for many products. On-site windshield repair services, computer repair pick up, and so on, are very popular as are any services that help customers avoid making a trip to a dealer or shop. Be creative in thinking of ways to make it easier for your customer.

- *Offer to handle the transaction efficiently.* For complex paperwork, say "You just fill in this part and I'll handle the rest." Be certain that you don't require unneeded or repetitive forms or application items from customers.

- *Take a trade-in (or dispose of old products for the customer).* This is especially important if you are selling something bulky or difficult to dispose of like mattresses or appliances.

- *Offer to handle additional details.* ("I'll get your license forms taken care of for you.")

- *Make your Web site or phone handling efficient.* Remember that people who buy online have the attention span of a gnat. Make the Web site exceptionally friendly and easy to use. Have sufficient staff to handle incoming phone calls so that you can answer on the first ring.

PART IV

POWERFUL IDEAS
FOR SAVING POSSIBLE
LOST CUSTOMERS

Any company can give adequate customer service when everything goes well. A smooth transaction is easy. But when glitches occur, when customers have problems or are even a little bit disappointed, the great companies quickly distinguish themselves. Service recovery is also best accomplished when seen as an opportunity rather than a painful chore.

Granted, most of us would prefer to not hear about customers' dissatisfaction. That's human nature. But given that dissatisfaction is inevitable, see recovery as an opportunity and challenge.

Customer complaints are opportunities to cement relationships. The vast majority of such relationships are worth saving, although occasionally—I stress *occasionally*—we need to let go of the chronic complainer. The tips in this section show ways to recover potentially lost customers.

IDEA 29.
KEEP IN TOUCH.

An athletic-shoe store and a rental car agency are good examples of this simple idea. A week after purchasing some running shoes, customers receive a handwritten note from the store owner simply thanking them for buying. Without fancy prose, it expresses appreciation for their business and invites them to return.

An airport car rental agency has employees write thank-you notes to customers when the desk is not busy. The notes are handwritten and personalized to mention the type of car rented. They thank the customers and invite them to rent again the next time they are in town.

Don't let your customer forget you.

Another way to not let customers forget you is to send them information about upcoming sales, changes in policies, new promotions, and so on. Keep the customer tied in.

Discount coupons or special hours for preferred customers are often appreciated.

A print shop sends all customers a monthly package of coupons, flyers, and samples including a printed motivated quote on parchment paper suitable for framing. Additional copies of the quote are available free for the asking. The mailing acts as a reminder of the quality of work the shop can do as well as a promotion.

In today's networked world, keeping in touch is increasingly important. Just having a current list of customers is a valuable asset. For example, a tactic being used by colleges and universities to keep in touch with their alumni is to give them lifetime e-mail addresses. The address may read GeorgeSmith@MajorUniversity.edu or BarbaraJones @Stanfordalumni.org. Taking this idea a step further, some colleges offer forwarding accounts that will automatically forward e-mail to an alumnus's primary e-mail account. The benefit to the school, of course, is that it can better keep in touch with alumni by always knowing how to reach them. This information can be used for fund raising as well as other information sharing.[1]

The costs of offering e-mail addresses is minimal; it amounts to little more than a basic Web-based account similar to the sort offered free by Yahoo! or Hotmail. However, it can be a valuable and innovative way to keep in touch with customers.

IDEA 30.
RECOGNIZE THE VALUE OF INFORMATION AND GIVE CUSTOMERS THE BEST.

In today's information age, information in and of itself is being recognized more fully as a valuable commodity. Companies try to keep up with the information that will help them stay most competitive. They generate Web sites, ads, brochures, and countless other forms of information that they hope will make them stand out in the marketplace. They try to improve the information customers receive from face-to-face contact and telephone support with customer service representatives.

Every product or service offered has an information component that is required for people to gain its full benefit. A can of soup includes ingredients, nutrition information, and recipes. A quick lube center might give information about how often to do oil changes and how to make your car last longer. One way to build customer loyalty is by providing information that exceeds what customers anticipate. This means giving more and clearer information using different media that's better than your competition.

WHAT NOT TO DO WITH INFORMATION
Don't confuse or mislead customers with information. I recently ordered merchandise from a dot-com company that

sold vitamins. The company offered next-day delivery at no extra charge. Five days later, my order had not arrived and my e-mail to the company was unanswered. After a phone call, I received an e-mail a day later that simply referred to the products by their SKU (reference code) number, without even mentioning their names. The correspondence listed which SKUs had been shipped or were still "being processed," but offered no apology, no explanation, no estimate of arrival, not even a thank-you or the name of a person to contact.

Another e-tailer, an online florist, provided an example of how to excel with information. ProFlowers tells customers when ordered flowers were picked up by the local distributor, when delivered and who accepted the delivery. After ordering a gift wreath for my sister scheduled to arrive December 15, I received a telephone message on December 12 asking me to contact ProFlowers on their toll-free line about the order. A rep apologized for failing to fax the order to the distributor, advised me that my shipment would be one day late, and dropped the shipping charge.

SOME WAYS TO GIVE CUSTOMERS A-PLUS INFORMATION

↳ *Evaluate your current information.* Go through the documentation you already distribute and ask, "Is this user friendly? Clear? Memorable? Colorful?" Have customers and front-line service reps look at it and ask: "Can you understand this? Is it interesting? Clear? Memorable?" Spend time getting inside the shoes of the customer and make adjustments to your messages accordingly. Too often, we assume that the kinds of information we've been using is just fine, and often it is not.

↳ *Evaluate any new information pieces.* Ask the same questions before you put out any new piece of information. Run it by actual customers and frontline people first. Ask, "What might you understand about this? How might it be confusing? Is any terminology unclear? How would you rephrase the message if you were passing it on to someone else?"

↪ *Audit your company's written documents, telephone scripts, and presentations.* Hire a business communication expert from a local university. Even if you have created wonderful documentation once, reread materials occasionally. A year later, you and others may see new ways to improve them. Keep a mind-set where brainstorming new ideas for information improvement is a constant process.

As you audit information materials, use these guidelines for analyzing documents and presentations:

- Is the tone of the writing to the point or too abrupt?

- Do you use clichés or jargon? Will the customer comprehend the meaning of a term?

- Do you use stock numbers or abbreviations that you understand but customers don't?

- Do you express appreciation? Even when a letter is about a problem or delay, do you start off with a "thank you for ordering" or "thank you for your patience"?

- Do you offer an alternative to solve a problem, and tell customers what you can do, not just what you can't?

- Do you provide a reasonable explanation of why a policy exists, instead of just saying "It's against our policy"?

- Do you provide positive redundancy to insure the message is clearly communicated? Often, customers comprehend information more fully if you present it in verbal or written form and graphically, with pictures and diagrams. Manuals, reference charts, videos, online help, and 800-hotlines are all forms of redundancy that can improve customer satisfaction.

CHECK FOR EFFECTIVENESS, NOT MERE EFFICIENCY

When choosing which media to use to communicate with customers, consider what result you want to achieve. If your message is simple—a departmental sign, a memo about a price change, a cooking tip—using an inexpensive but efficient medium, such as a flyer, label, or instruction sheet is enough.

As messages grow more complex, effectiveness becomes more important. Communication effectiveness is achieved when the message is received by the right people, easily understood, remembered for a reasonable amount of time, and applied. The media that achieve this, most notably face-to-face contact, may be more costly and less efficient, but the customer satisfaction may be well worth the extra cost.

For example, Chevrolet provides audiotape owner's guides to teach customers about the features of cars and trucks. Continental Cablevision in St. Paul, Minnesota, has a program called "TV House Call" where a company representative demonstrates live the solution to an individual subscriber's problem while the customer watches.

Customer classes can be effective information tools as well. An auto repair shop stood out by offering classes on how consumers could maintain their cars. One class in particular targeted women and explained how each part of the car worked.

CONSIDER YOUR GRAPHICS, LAYOUT, SIGNAGE, AND ICONS

These supplement messages' words and make them clearer. With the onset of computer graphics and video games, people are that much more visual today. For example, a hospital reception area that was not staffed had color-coded tape on the floor to direct people to various areas.

Even simple instructions can be offered in innovative or accessible ways. I bought one sprinkler attachment that had instructions in cartoon form. It showed a person turning the hose on and getting sprayed in the face. Here was a $5 item offering information in a fun, memorable way.

SEEK OUT OPPORTUNITIES FOR E-COMMUNICATION

Surveys showed that 40 percent of e-commerce sites don't provide an e-mail address for customer questions and 75 percent don't post phone numbers. Another survey by e-tailer trade group *Shop.org* found that about one quarter of shoppers don't receive responses to their e-mailed requests for help.

Handle increased customer volume from the Web by providing answers to frequently asked questions (FAQs). Increase effectiveness by having one level that addresses the needs of prospects and new customers and another level for customers already familiar with products and services.

Webjump.com serves a half million customers without staff or budget to take customer support calls. Instead, it developed a dynamic FAQs section to handle most customer questions. One executive estimated it would cost $40 million a year to provide the same service by phone or e-mail.

MEASURE INFORMATION EFFORTS

Keep track of questions customers commonly ask in face-to-face and telephone conversations as well. If several people are asking the same questions or experiencing similar confusion, you have an information problem. Make it worthwhile for employees to record and pass on customer feedback by offering them incentives for listing customer comments. Teach customer service representatives to make notes of responses, even when they are face to face with customers. Customers will appreciate that they are being heard.

Create a survey that invites customers to describe the amount of information they receive when making informed decisions about your products or services. Have them rate on a scale of one to five the types of information they do receive as compared to what they need to receive. Cover these areas:

- Face-to-face contact with one employee.

- Face-to-face contact with two or more people.

- Telephone support.

- Product documentation, such as owner's manuals and instructions.

- Videos, audiotapes, and other electronic media.

- Online help, Web pages, and FAQs.

- Newsletters, information bulletins, and fact sheets.

Just as with other types of service, the more effectively you anticipate and go beyond customer's expectations for information, the more you build customer loyalty and add value to the products and services they buy from your company.

 IDEA 31.
MASTER RECOVERY SKILLS.

Only you can be the judge of whether a customer is worth saving. But, if you read the beginning of this book, you'll recognize the tremendous cost of replacing a customer. So why not try to save the ones you have? To do so, use "recovery" skills.

Recognize that upset customers want some or all of the following from you:

- To be listened to and taken seriously.

- To understand their problem and the reason they are upset.

- Compensation or restitution.

- A sense of urgency; to get their problem handled quickly.

- Avoidance of further inconvenience.

- To be treated with respect.

- To have someone punished for the problem.

- Assurance that the problem will not happen again.

When dealing with an upset customer, try this approach:

1. *Empathize with the customer's problem.* Don't jump to defend yourself or your company. If a customer says he has a problem, he does. Work with him; don't debate the point. I experienced a good example of this when calling an auto dealership's repair shop. I told the service manager that although I had just had my car in for a repair, the car was showing the same symptoms as before they worked on it. I expected a debate but instead got an immediate positive comment. The service manager said, "Oh, oh, sounds like we need to get that fixed for you quick-like." He immediately focused on the problem, not on debating whose fault it was.

2. *Apologize for the situation.* Even if it isn't your fault, you can express regret that *the situation* came up. "I'm sorry you're upset" can help deflate the customer's anger or frustration.

3. *State that you want to help.* "Let's see what we can do to get this fixed."

4. *Probe for information.* Keep this discussion impersonal; don't blame anyone. "You didn't do that right" will just start a fight, while "this application needs to be completed before the account can be set up" stays impersonal and doesn't cast blame.

5. *Explain options that could solve the problem*s. Then ask what they would like to have happen. "We can either cancel the original order and resubmit a new one , or . . . Which would you like to do?"

6. *Summarize the action you will take and tell them that you value their business.* If done correctly, this should make for a pleasant ending that will linger with the customer. And don't forget the thank-you.

If all goes well, you should feel a genuine sense of satisfaction after handling an unhappy or irate customer. But this is not a perfect world and people are not always rational, so sometimes you too get upset. Maintain your composure, your dignity, and your professionalism.

If the encounter doesn't work out as well as you'd hoped, keep these things in mind:

↪ If you *tried your best to satisfy* the customer, you have done all that you can do.

↪ Upset people often say things they don't really mean. *Don't take it personally.* They are blowing off steam, venting frustration. If the problem was really your fault, resolve to learn from the experience and do better next time. If you had no control over the situation, do what you can, but don't bang your head against the wall.

↪ Once you have handled the situation, it's done. *Don't rehash the experience* with your co-workers or in your own mind. Recounting the experience with others probably won't make their day any better and rehashing it to yourself will just make you mad. You may, however, want to ask another person how he or she would have handled the situation.

↪ Every customer contact experience is an *opportunity to improve* your professionalism. Even the most unpleasant encounter can teach you useful lessons. Vow to learn for each one.

When the situation has cooled, you may want to review with an eye toward improving your skills. Think back on the situation in which you used your recovery skills and ask questions such as these:

▪ What was the nature of the customer's complaint?

▪ How did the customer see the problem? Who was to blame, what irritated him most, why was she angry or frustrated?

- How did you see the problem? Was the customer partially to blame?

- What did you say to the customer that helped the situation?

- What did you say that seemed to aggravate the situation?

- How did you show your concern to the customer?

- How did you apply your communication skills?

- How did you demonstrate your competence?

- What would you do differently?

- Do you think this customer will do business with you again? Why or why not?

IDEA 32.
DISARM THE CHRONIC COMPLAINER.

"Stubbornness is the energy of fools," says the German proverb. Sometimes we need to draw the line between upset customers with legitimate problems and chronic complainers who consume our time with unreasonable demands—the dreaded "customers from hell."

Step one in dealing with such people is to be sure the person really is a *chronic* complainer. When you've tried the normal recovery approaches and nothing seems to work, look for the following telltale signs:[2]

- *They always look for someone to blame.* In their worlds, nothing is an accident: Someone is always at fault, and it's probably you.

- *They never admit any degree of fault or responsibility.* They see themselves as blameless and victims of the incompetence or malice of others.

- *They have strong ideas about what others should do.* They love to define other peoples' duties. If you hear a complaint phrased exclusively in terms of what other people *always, never, must,* or *must not* do, chances are you're talking to a chronic complainer.

- *They complain at length.* While normal complainers pause for breath every now and then, chronics seem able to inhale while saying the words, "and another thing . . ."

When faced with that occasional chronic complainer (they really are quite rare, fortunately), try these techniques:

- *Active listening* to identify the legitimate grievance beneath the endless griping. Rephrase the complainers main points in your own words, even if you have to interrupt to do so. Say something like, "Excuse me, but do I understand you to say that the package didn't arrive on time and you feel frustrated and annoyed?"

- *Establish the facts* to reduce the complainer's tendency to exaggerate or overgeneralize. If he says "I tried calling all day but as usual you tried to avoid me," establish the actual number of times called and when.

- *Resist the temptation to apologize,* although that may seem to be the natural thing to do. Because the main thing the complainer is trying to do is fix blame—not solve problems—your apology will be seen as an open invitation to further blaming. Instead, ask questions: "Would an extended warranty solve your problem?" or "When would be the best time for me to call you back with that information?"

- *Get the complainer to pose solutions* to the problem, especially if he doesn't seem to like your ideas. Also, try putting a time limit on the conversation by saying something like, "I have to talk with someone in 10 minutes. What sort of action plan can we work out in that time?" The object of this is to get him away from whining and into a problem-solving mode.

We have, of course, no guarantees when dealing with such customers, but the effort may well be worth it. Converting one of these folks into a normal, rational customer can be professionally rewarding.

IDEA 33.
RECONCILE CUSTOMER GOODWILL WITH "SYMBOLIC ATONEMENT."

When attempting to recover an unhappy customer, the icing on the cake is the "something extra" you give by way of making up for the problem.

Suppose you buy a new pair of shoes and the heel falls off. You call the shoe store and the owner says to bring them back and he'll replace them. You take time off from work, drive downtown to the store, battle for a parking space, and spend about an hour doing this. He cheerfully gives you a new pair of shoes. Are you satisfied now?

Probably not. Why? Because he really hasn't repaid you for the inconvenience. Sure, he stood behind the product and perhaps even did so in a pleasant manner, but you still came out on the short end.

What kinds of things can we do for "symbolic atonement"—to be seen as going the extra mile in the eyes of a customer? Some of these may work:

- *Offer to pick up or deliver* goods to be replaced or repaired. This is especially important in cases where the customer suffers from a defective product or service from you.

- *Give a gift* of merchandise or a gift certificate to repay for the inconvenience. The gift may be small but the thought will be appreciated.

- *Reimburse* customers for costs of returning merchandise such as parking fees, and so on. (Mail-order retailers pay all return postage fees to reduce customer dissatisfaction.)

- At the very minimum, *acknowledge* the customer's inconvenience and thank him for coming back.

Toyota's Lexus division did a good job of handling a product recall shortly after coming onto the market with its new line of luxury cars. This was the company's initial entry into the luxury car market with the new Lexus line. Much to the company's embarrassment, it became necessary to recall a large number of automobiles for a minor product defect. But Lexus turned lemons into lemonade. Dealers called customers for an appointment to pick up the car. They left a loaner car, and some dealers left "symbolic atonement" in the form of a rose or a $50 bill on the seat to apologize for the inconvenience. The outcome: Customers were exposed to the dealership's exceptional (and profitable) service department. What started as an embarrassment became what one Toyota executive called "a watershed event" for getting customers into the dealer's shop.

If you are a manager, be certain to empower your people to do these kinds of things. Let your people give away a little when appropriate. Give them guidelines about appropriate give-away behaviors and lead by example.

PART V

POWERFUL IDEAS
MANAGERS CAN USE TO GET
EMPLOYEE INVOLVEMENT

Managers face special challenges in creating customer loyalty. While most effective managers recognize its importance and do these things themselves, they also have the added responsibility of getting other people (employees) to do the kinds of things that lead to happy, loyal customers.

In this section, you'll find some powerful ideas on how managers can fulfill their special roles.

IDEA 34.
GET EVERYONE INVOLVED IN SETTING
A THEME.

When I consult with organizations, I typically ask if they have a customer service theme or credo. Fairly often I get answers such as: "Oh, yes, we have 13 points to excellent customer service." I'd reply, "Oh, really? What's point 11?" The manager would say, "Well, I don't know exactly." Then I'd ask, "Well, how about point 6? Which one's that?" And he says, "I'm not sure, I actually haven't memorized all these things, but we have these points posted around the office."

That's not good enough for today's competitive environment. Identifying a theme means to come up with a succinct, clear statement of what the organization is about and how it could be seen as unique in the eyes of the customer.

Let's go through that one more time. An effective credo or theme must be:

- Succinct.

- Clear.

- Descriptive of uniqueness.

The reason you want it succinct and clear is so that every employee can remember and "buy into" this as a guiding statement that will shape their actions and help them make decisions. As I tell my consulting clients, the credo needs to be so memorable that employees can repeat it at gunpoint.

Let's look at a couple of examples:

Federal Express, the package delivery service, has a simple, clear theme. In fact, the company expresses it in three words: "Absolutely, positively, overnight." It will get the packages there absolutely, positively, overnight, and it's 99.8 percent successful at doing that. The highly successful Ritz-Carlton hotel chain has a simple credo: They see all their employees as "ladies and gentlemen helping ladies and gentlemen."

A *Harvard Business Review*[1] article told of a Seattle restaurant staff who wrestled with this idea of a simple, clear theme. After carefully looking at the company through the eyes of their customer, asking, "Just what does our restaurant guest want from us?" They came up with this theme: "Your enjoyment guaranteed. Always." That is exactly what they offer their guests: enjoyment.

A neat thing about this simple theme was that people could buy into it, and in fact they made it into an acronym: YEGA. While YEGA may not mean anything to most of us, it became a catchword for their organization. They developed YEGA promotions and YEGA bucks and YEGA pins and hats to get their employees involved in the spirit of YEGA. It was fun, it was interesting, and it reminded the employees constantly of that simple four-word theme: "Your enjoyment guaranteed. Always."

Here is how to articulate a good theme:

- *Commit* to work on the process of identifying a customer-focused theme. Remember, this needs to be from the customer's viewpoint, not necessarily yours. Making great profits may be a company goal, but it would not be a good customer credo.

- Make it *succinct, clear, and descriptive* of your uniqueness. It should allude to what makes you and your organization different.

- *Gather ideas from your customers*. Ask them, "What five things do you want when doing business with us?" Ask them to respond quickly off the top of their heads, and look at the language that they use. Their own wording may be significant.

- Similarly, gather your own people together in the organization and ask, *"If you were our customer, what five things would you like to get from a company like ours?"* Ask people to respond quickly. Jot down the language and then collect all of the words. (Quick listing often gets to target words more effectively than long descriptions.)

As you gather perceptions from customers and employees, you'll notice that some terms come up over and over again. These typically are the kinds of words that will resonate with your customer. These are good words to put into your customer service theme.

As you draft a theme for your organization, remember:

- You will probably have to go through several versions and do some wordsmithing to make it just right. Don't jump to the first idea and don't use cliches.

- Participation and input from customers and employees is very important. The customers can best tell you what they're looking for in an organization like yours, and the employees' participation will ensure that they will accept the theme.

- Write several rough drafts of the theme; don't be too quick to come up with the finished version. Phrase the final version in 10 words or fewer.

- If possible, try to make the theme into an acronym, where the first letters of each word form a word in themselves. For example, one computer company launched a program called CARE, which stood for "Customers Are Really Everything." The YEGA example I gave earlier is another example of an acronym.

When you've identified a statement of uniqueness, ask yourself if everyone in the organization would choose roughly the same words you chose to describe this distinctiveness. A simple way to verify this is to grab some of your employees and ask them to describe the organization's theme. Especially invite an employee who's been with the organization for 10 days or less to identify the theme.

"What good does it do just to be able to repeat such a phrase?" The answer is that it's a start. Repeating some words may seem meaningless at first, but most organizations fall far short even of that level of agreement. Focusing your people on a common theme is well worth the effort.

The ideal theme, according to Tom Peters in his book, *Thriving on Chaos*, should meet the following criteria. It has to be:

1. Roughly right.

2. Enduring.

3. Succinct.

4. Memorable.

5. Believable.

6. Energizing to all.

Do not feel that, as a manger, you must define this theme alone. That can be a formula for disaster. If employees feel that this is some slogan that's being rammed down their throats, they will not buy into it. By having employees participate in clarifying a theme, they will feel more committed to it. This has been shown time and again since the earliest studies in human relations. Front-line people know the customers best and can give great ideas on how to better serve them. Never overlook the ideas of this group of experts. The employees on the firing line have good ideas. Use them.

One final note: A theme is not necessarily forever. As an organization changes directions, as markets or economic conditions change, a theme may be modified. Some organizations may want to use a theme statement for a limited period of time much the way advertisers use a slogan for only a few years. Modifying the theme should not, however, be done without careful thought. Consistency of direction is in itself valuable.

IDEA 35.
REWARD THE RIGHT ACTIONS.

The reward system within an organization needs to be tilted to the advantage of the employee who provides excellent service. Any rewards should be given in direct relationship to the employee's contribution to customer service consistent with the theme you've selected. Rewards take many forms, some obvious, some more subtle:

- Salary and cash bonuses.

- Prizes and awards.

- Promotions and job enrichment (giving employees additional responsibilities).

- Preferred work locations, better offices, larger desks.

- Work scheduling flexibility (preferred hours, job sharing).

- Pins, badges, uniforms, award patches.

- Reserved parking spaces or mass transit passes.

- "Employee of the week (or month)" recognition.

- Compliments, spoken and (better yet) in writing.

- Surprise recognition parties or celebrations.

- Lunches or banquets.

- Newsletter write-ups.

Management is only limited by its imagination when it comes to rewarding employees. But the most important point is that *managers reward the right actions and results.*

Avoid rewarding one behavior while hoping for something else. In all too many cases an organization *hopes* something will happen but actually rewards an opposite behavior. This is a widespread problem.

Here are some examples of counterproductive uses of rewards:

⤷ Rewarding individuals and departments for *not* receiving complaints. The hope is that by receiving no complaints it means we are doing a good job. The reality, however, may well be that no complaints are heard because the complaints are simply being suppressed. Customers have no effective way to voice a complaint. Instead, they just quit doing business with the company.

⤷ Rewarding employees only for fast transaction handling when the customer may be left uninformed or may resent being rushed along. A restaurant that encourages employees to get the customer fed and out may create unhappy customers who prefer to eat more slowly. The electronic equipment buyer who does not understand how to work the features of a product but feels rushed and fails to ask.

⤷ Encouraging salespeople to "cooperate with each other to best meet the customer needs" while paying a straight commission. Example: Salespeople practically trip over each other to approach the new customer before the other guy gets him.

⤷ Encouraging employees to send thank-you notes to customers but never allowing on-the-job time to do so. (This creates the impression that it really isn't that important.)

⤷ Constantly stressing the need to reduce the amount of return merchandise by docking the pay of clerks who accept too many returns. Result: Customers encounter reluctance to take back unsatisfactory products.

⤷ Paying people by the hour instead of by the task accomplished. Hourly wages are simpler to administer, but they basically pay people for using up time! Be more creative. Give bonuses for accomplishments, not just for taking time.

Check your organization. Are you really rewarding the right behaviors?

IDEA 36.
TRAIN AND RETRAIN TO BUILD EMPLOYEE
COMPETENCE.

Competence is the knowledge and skills needed to anticipate, identify, and satisfy customer needs. Excellent customer service people work to continually learn and grow. They know how important it is to keep current about their organization, products, services, and procedures. They know that they alone are ultimately responsible for upgrading their skills and increasing their value and professionalism.

The situation below, as written up by the editor of an investment magazine distributed to thousands of readers, clearly illustrates the problem of low competence:

> One day last month I went to buy a cordless drill. At the first store I tried, I was encouraged when I immediately found one that seemed suitable. When I went to pay for it, however, I found that it did not have a price tag. To make matters worse, not a single clerk was in sight.[2]

The author goes on to describe how she overheard a clerk telling another customer that they could probably get the item they wanted from a competitor, and that he could get a discount there as well!

> When I asked for help, she said, "Well, that's not really my department." But she finally agreed and spent the next 10 minutes poking through an unruly pile of merchandise that bore not the faintest resemblance to the item I sought.

Later, the department manager came bustling out to help. After more fruitless searching, he offered to sell the writer the sample if she "thought $39.95 was a reasonable price." This caused the writer to wonder:

Shouldn't prices be set by some higher authority, I thought? Didn't barter go out with agrarian societies? Desperate to get out of the store, I agreed.

When she went to the register to pay for the item, the clerk punched in the product code number, and found that the price was $69.95. When the customer said she didn't want the merchandise, the clerk said, "Yeah, I don't blame you—too expensive."

And so ended another excruciating hour of shopping at an establishment where the customer comes last.

Contrast that story with one where competence is stressed. The efforts of a chain of athletic footwear and clothing stores was written up for its efforts to improve competence:

"... the company put all its store managers through a 12-to-18-month, soup-to-nuts training process. Employees learn about every aspect of the operation from the structure of the foot and the basics of bookkeeping to techniques for closing a sale and selling to children. And that's not all. Each store is also equipped with a VCR, the better to play a series of specialized training videotapes. Store managers also receive sports-medicine books so they can become familiar with the health problems of their customers."[3]

The difference is the emphasis on training and retraining. Where would you rather shop?

Training cannot be a one-shot affair.

People quickly forget ideas taught to them in training sessions. Repeated exposures to the same ideas are almost always necessary for people to apply those ideas. Training cannot be a one-shot affair. It cannot be a once-a-year retreat. Training must be ongoing.

Training need not always be formal, classroom sessions. Often the best training happens in small groups or one-to-one communication among associates in an organization.

When I worked as a manager for a public utility, we found the best results occurred when supervisors spent about 10 minutes each morning before opening to the public to remind service representatives of the skills and behaviors they needed to apply. Like a coach warming up a star athlete, the good supervisor will train and retrain on a regular basis.

Remember, too, that training is much more than just telling. It involves hands-on practice, critiques, and regular follow-up. For example, a restaurant assigns an experienced, successful server to "shadow" the newer employee, observing and helping. The newer employee benefits from the critique and the comfort of knowing that the backup can help out if a problem arises. The experienced server feels a sense of contribution from the mini-management role.

How to know what kind of training to provide

Most employees tasks fall within their scope of ability, but in some cases they don't know what to do. To broaden their professional competence, they need to find the answers and try out new skills.

Managers should do regular needs assessments. Encourage employees to list questions they have or skills they'd like to sharpen or learn. Have them answer the following question for each the three categories described:

What more information or additional skills would you like to know about:

1. The company, department, or organization's procedures?

2. The products and services we sell?

3. Handling customers effectively?

Encourage people to share their list with supervisors and jointly make a plan to get the training and experience needed.

Training builds competence. Customers gain a sense of confidence and reassurance as they watch expert employees at work.

IDEA 37.
EXPLAIN THE TABOOS IN NO UNCERTAIN
TERMS.

Managers should make clear from the first day of employment that there are specific taboos: things that are simply not to be done in our organization. Sometimes people are uncomfortable telling people about these things; they hate to focus on the negative—but it must be done. Do not assume that all employees will always use good common sense nor that they recognize certain behaviors as inappropriate in the workplace. Better to be explicit when orienting an employee than have to correct them later.

For example, in a supermarket, checkout clerks are told repeatedly of this taboo: They must absolutely *avoid chatting with each other about personal matters when a customer is present.* This supermarket placed special emphasis on this taboo because it recently reinstated baggers at all the checkout counters. (A few years ago, it was fashionable to have the customers bag their own groceries and thus save a little bit of money. But customers have changed and people now want to have the groceries packaged for them.) The new procedure now calls for two people at each cash register, a checker and a bagger. The danger in this is that the checker and bagger, often young people, enjoy each other's company and may find themselves talking to each other and ignoring the customer. Therefore, management simply told each employee that if there are no customers around it's okay to chat while you're working, but when the customer appears, all personal discussions and chit-chat must stop. That is one of the taboos.

In other organizations, taboos may include:
- Never make fun of a customer (no subtle sarcasm or behind-their-back joking).
- Never accept a tip or gratuity from a customer.

- Never respond sarcastically to a customer comment.

- Never sit down on the job.

- Never allow the phone to interrupt a face-to-face conversation with a customer.

- Never degrade a competitor's product, a customer's trade-in, a customer's expressed preference, and so on.

Taboos are the "shalt not's" of customer service. Keep the list of taboos reasonably short but be sure they are consistently enforced.

 IDEA 38.
PROVIDE THE RIGHT STUFF AND ADEQUATE BREAKS.

Some companies are providing business cards for every employee, even those at the lowest organizational levels. Clerks or entry-level people especially enjoy having a business card. It makes them feel valued and part of the team. For a few dollars invested, managers can generate good feelings in employees.

In addition, employees cannot effectively deliver good service without proper tools. Be sure your customer-contact people have the tools to do their jobs. Can everyone who needs one find:

- A telephone in a place where it can be heard? Telephone headsets for people who use the phone heavily?

- A computer with quick access to customer records?

- A fax machine or messenger service? Packing supplies for overnight delivery services?

- Letterhead, envelopes, postage?

- Business cards and/or personalized stationery?

- Product information and publications? Samples?

- Easy access to policy and procedure statements?

- A desk, writing table, or place to confer with customers?

- Office supplies?

- A mobile or portable phone?

- A decent break area where employees can relax and recharge?

Customer service to meet today's challenge needs today's equipment.

ALLOW ADEQUATE WORK BREAKS

Also, be sure that your customer-contact people get adequate breaks. Did you know that most Las Vegas dealers work 20-minute shifts. How long do your people work with customers?

Customer contact work can be some of the most emotionally demanding labor imaginable. To stay sharp and do it right, people need breaks. They need time to complete paperwork or just work in an environment away from people. Especially when things are hectic, try to schedule a break or a diversion (other work that gets them away from customers) regularly.

No one can keep totally cool and mentally alert indefinitely. To paraphrase Vince Lombardi, "Fatigue makes cowards (and grouches!) of us all."

IDEA 39.
CONSTANTLY RECRUIT GREAT PEOPLE.

Steal good employees. As you come across people with great attitudes and excellent customer service skills, try to hire them away or at least recommend them to your boss. Start a file of people you'd like to have working for you and when an opening occurs, contact them.

Don't worry if they are working in a totally different type of business. The specifics of your organization can be taught. Great attitudes cannot.

One owner of a chain of fast-food restaurants (an industry where employee turnover is high) routinely passes out his business card to customer-contact people who give him good service. He tells them that if ever they consider a job change, please call him directly. That has got to be impressive to people—to be invited to call the owner directly.

People are flattered when you invite them to work with you. Even if they don't accept your job offer, they will get the message that you are looking for the best people available because you value excellent service-givers.

Being on the lookout for good potential employees should be an ongoing task for all managers. And, getting your employees involved can pay off too. Invite all employees to become recruiters. Your best hires may well be referred to you from people who already work with you.

IDEA 40.
NURTURE A CULTURE OF CARING.

What is an organizational culture? It's a whole set of values, attitudes, and ways of doing things that are generally accepted by organization leaders and members. The culture defines rules of behavior, written and unwritten, that employees are expected to live by. Without such a set of rules and norms, employees become confused and ineffective, like a foreigner traveling in a strange country. Ignorance of cultural norms inevitably leads to mistakes or inappropriate behaviors.

An organization's culture is not something that can be "put in place" by decree. A culture emerges over a period of time and is nurtured. So don't try to rush the process. If you have done a good job in developing a credo or service theme, you have gone a long way toward defining the culture.

For the culture to support a value of caring about customers, several factors are necessary:

1. The company cannot just give lip service to customer care. Top leaders must sincerely feel and believe in it.

2. Leaders must take the long view. Giving exceptional customer service may not provide an immediate return.

3. Employees must be involved at all organizational levels.

4. Ongoing training must reinforce the company's values.

5. Rewards must reinforce behaviors that support the culture.

6. The taboos must be explicit.

7. The organization must engage in some hoopla and fun (for this reinforces the group commitment).

Managers, how does your organization measure up? Do your people have a sense of the culture? If not, start discussions with them to help articulate the factors above.

IDEA 41.
ENRICH PEOPLE'S JOBS.

As we carefully observe what people are doing and reward appropriate behaviors, we start to grow service champions, people who become real advocates of your customers.

The best indicator of whether a person is a service champion is to view who they are working for. Given the choice, you are better off with someone who works first for the customer and second for the company. These people are your champions. This isn't really an either-or choice; serving the customer *is* serving the company, so long as the employee doesn't give away the store.

Managers need to recognize champion potential and cultivate it. Here are some ways to identify and grow potential champs:

- Look for people with "task maturity," that is, those who have good potential business sense. Note: This kind of maturity has nothing to do with age. Instead, it results from the individual's:

1. Ability to set ambitious but attainable goals.

2. Willingness and capability to take responsibility for his or her results and actions.

3. Experience and/or education relevant to the job they are doing.

4. Personal self-confidence, self-respect, and general good judgment.

People with these characteristics become the best candidates for growth on the job.

- Give the "mature" employee additional authority to act on behalf of the customer. Example: The company previously has a blanket rule that any refund of more than $10 must be approved by a manager. When service champions are identified, allow them to handle their own approvals. Other areas where the "mature" employee may be given additional authority might be:

  1. Approving unusual orders or exceptions to the "normal" customer requests.

  2. Authorizing home delivery of merchandise or pickup of defective products.

  3. Approving checks or other methods of payment.

  4. Scheduling work times, breaks, and lunch hours.

  5. Making unsolicited customer follow-up calls.

  6. Suggesting different compensation, bonus systems, or special promotions.

  7. Participation in merchandise buying decisions.

  8. Monitoring or training newer employees.

These and other forms of job enrichment build service champions by rewarding them with additional job freedom and opportunity to take initiative.

When employees truly feel free to be an advocate for their customer, they begin to give exemplary service that goes beyond what the customer expects.

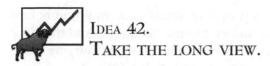

IDEA 42.
TAKE THE LONG VIEW.

Motivational speakers cite the example of a bamboo tree that must be watered and fertilized for years while no noticeable growth takes place. Then, after years of nurturing, the bamboo tree shoots up as much as 18 or 20 feet in a few weeks. All the nourishment and care pays off in an incredible growth spurt. Such can be the case with excellent service. The results may be delayed, but the work will surely pay off.

Just as the impact of one lost customer is not felt immediately, so the impact of an ongoing improvement program takes time to mature. Recognizing that a lost customer is not just a few dollars a week in income, but rather thousands or tens of thousands of dollars over a period of years, is one example of the long view.

Think too of the pressure a poor-service organization places on its workers: the psychological cost of the unhappy patron or customer on employees. People working with disgruntled or even outraged customers day after day pay a terrible price in terms of stress and job dissatisfaction. While the impact may not be immediate, by taking the long view we soon recognize the costs in employee attitudes, health, absenteeism, and eventual turnover.

Changing employee behavior takes time. Changing customer perceptions of an organization can take even longer. Service improvement programs need to be phased in and stuck with even though they don't appear to bear immediate fruit.

In the short run, when organizations tackle a particular customer problem, they may, by digging into the nature of the problem, find that things seem to get worse: They receive *more* complaints and apparently more dissatisfied customers initially. This is not a deteriorating situation but simply better measurements of the extent of the problem.

As the company improves methods and employee behaviors, the number of customer complaints drops. And this drop is a real improvement, not an illusion created by burying heads in the sand. Take the long view and stick with it.

IDEA 43.
RECOGNIZE AND REINFORCE GREAT SERVICE.

Catch your people doing things right. Also, let them know they've been caught!

Too many managers seem to focus on looking for mistakes and jumping down the throat of those who commit them. The problem with such an approach is that it focuses on exactly the wrong thing. Here's why: What we focus on grows—we get more of it. If a manager keeps looking for screw-ups, he or she will find more and more of them.

If managers want good customer behaviors to grow in our organization, they need to focus on the positive things happening and then reinforce the effective behaviors "caught."

In doing so, don't underestimate the power of simple rewards. Few things are as powerful as praise or verbal reinforcement given appropriately and immediately. If your people are doing the kinds of things you want them to be doing—they are serving the customers in an appropriate and exemplary way—they need to be thanked and appreciated.

In catching people doing things right and rewarding those behaviors, we create a sense of pride in the organization. People will feel better about their jobs, and will be more likely to stick with the company.

Managers have often misunderstood what is actually rewarding to employees. A national survey[4] asked workers to state the top 10 things they wanted most from their jobs in order of importance. At the same time, managers were asked to state their guesses of what the employees would find most important. Here are the surprising results:

Job Factors That Matter Most To Employees		
	Manager's Guess	Worker's Rating
1. Appreciation for good work	8	1
2. Feeling "in" on things	10	2
3. Help with personal problems	9	3
4. Job security	2	4
5. Good wages	1	5
6. Work that keeps you interested	5	6
7. Possibility for promotion	3	7
8. Personal loyalty to company or boss	6	8
9. Good working conditions	4	9
10. Tactful discipline	7	10

What does this have to do with catching and rewarding? It suggests that what managers have traditionally regarded as the best rewards may be only a small portion of the available reinforcers managers can use. It also shows that the simplest, most inexpensive reward—mere recognition—may be the most powerful reward of all. The single, most effective way to reward workers is to tell them how much you appreciate what they do. To give such compliments impact, make them:

↳ *Direct and specific.* Address them personally and tell them why you are pleased with what they've done. Example: "Tom, you did a really nice job of handling that situation with Mrs. Burton. I think she feels good about us and will probably be back as a customer. Thanks." Or: "Brenda, you did a really good job of picking up on that customer's disappointment. Most people would have just let her go unhappy, but you sensed that something was wrong and you fixed it. That's great customer service. Thanks."

↳ *Unconditionally positive.* Don't slip in a "left-handed compliment" or any comment that diminishes the praise. Avoid: "Marge, you sure handled Mr. Johnson's problem nicely—for once you actually sold him something too!" Or: "You kept your cool, Don. Those antidepressant drugs must be working for you. Keep up the good work." Or: "Nice sale, Harry. Can we talk about your order screw-up after lunch?"

Awareness of what employees want in their job helps managers create other forms of reward. For example, the study mentioned that workers want to feel "in" on things. A form of reward for great customer service, then, might be to invite a worker to serve on a decision-making committee (be sure this isn't just additional work piled on top of what he's already expected to do). Or, simply confiding in the worker about future plans can be rewarding. Example: "Ron, you seem to have a real feel for what the customers expect from us. I'd appreciate you reaction to this idea we've been kicking around about a home-delivery service. Would you help us think this through?"

While it is important to let your people know when they've been caught doing things right, we don't always know. Managers cannot be everywhere. Heroic deeds may often go virtually unnoticed despite best efforts to recognize and reward. And sometimes, it's difficult to adequately reinforce people during the heat of the battle.

An interesting approach used by companies to delivering reinforcement involves giving employees a card or "coupon" to let them know their work has been recognized. The giver of the card (either a customer or associate within the company) fills in the name of the employee and gives the card to him or her. The employee turns in the cards to a manager or sends them to the corporate offices where they can be exchanged for gifts and prizes.

CONGRATULATIONS

_____

You have just been caught

giving great service.

_____

Signature   Title   Date

American and Delta Airlines do a similar promotion sending coupons to their regular customers (frequent flyers). The cards could be given to any AA employee who performed exemplary service. (If your organization has a regular customer base, an approach that allows the customers to pass out the "rewards" can be particularly effective.) Again, the coupons were redeemed for awards.

IDEA 44.
TRACK CUSTOMER SERVICE BEHAVIORS
OVER TIME.

Keep track of evaluation scores and observations over a period of time to create an ongoing emphasis on service excellence. Without ongoing measures and tracking, customer service becomes no more than a short-term "program."

Among the scores that could be tracked are:

- Average scores received on shopper surveys.

- Number of customer complaints received and how quickly handled. Don't try to *eliminate* complaints; that may just suppress them.

- Number of company-initiated calls to customers to assess satisfaction.

- Company accessibility: How many times customers experience a busy signal or long lines.

- Random observations of employee behaviors. Count such things as eye contact time, smiling, efficiency of handling transactions, courtesy, thanking customers, and so on. Note the term "random" does not mean haphazard. Carefully plan such measurements so that any employee has an equal chance of being systematically observed.

TRACK A CUSTOMER LOYALTY INDEX[5]

Perhaps the most useful measure is one of the simplest. A Customer Loyalty Index can be easily calculated and tracked. Based on the key elements I described back in Idea 1 (page 15), you need to get responses to only three questionnaire items. Invite customers to respond on a five-point scale ranging from "strongly disagree" to "strongly agree" as follows:

1 = strongly disagree
2 = disagree
3 = neither agree nor disagree
4 = agree
5 = strongly agree

The three key statements are:

1. Overall, I am satisfied with my experience with XYZ Corporation.   1   2   3   4   5

2. I intend to continue to do business with XYZ Corporation as the need arises.   1   2   3   4   5

3. I would recommend XYZ Corporation to my family or friends.   1   2   3   4   5

Follow each statement with a five-point scale that customers can quickly circle. Gather a sufficient sample of customer responses and calculate average scores. (Add the total of all scores for each item and divide by the number or responses received. Carry the number out to two decimal points.) Then track any movement in the scores over time to indicate how you are doing in creating customer loyalty. Higher numbers indicate progress; a lower average indicates some erosion in loyalty. Don't panic over small changes, but do track the scores for a period of time. Some of my client organizations gather a random sample each month; some prefer a quarterly measure.

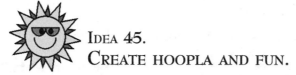

IDEA 45.
CREATE HOOPLA AND FUN.

As a customer, I bet you can tell when people are having fun at work. The best employers are ones that not only allow people to have fun, but encourage it. From countless small entrepreneurial businesses to industry giants like Southwest Airlines, Wal-Mart, Home Depot, and thousands of other successful companies, you'll find people enjoying their work, having fun.

On the flip side, I have been in businesses (a particular fast-food outlet comes to mind) where management must have passed a law against smiling! I stepped to the counter in that restaurant, smiled, and said hello, only to have the un-smiling clerk ask, in a monotone voice, "To stay or to go?" Gee, I'm sure glad I came in here. Your enthusiasm makes my whole day!

People enjoy working in an organization that's fun. Many organizations have regular rituals, whether it may be Friday afternoon popcorn, birthday parties, or employee-of-the-month celebrations, that everyone gets involved in. In the classic management book, *In Search of Excellence,* Tom Peters and Robert Waterman talk about the importance of hoopla and fun. Excellent organizations are fun places to work; they create rituals of their own.

As a manager at a utility company, I initiated frequent sales contests, complete with skits and prizes. Each time a particular product was sold, the service representative could pop a balloon and find inside of that balloon a prize ranging from a $10 bill to a coupon good for a piece of pie in the company cafeteria. Employees loved it and got involved.

Other ideas:

- Employee (or hero) of the week/month recognition.

- Recognition awards luncheons (include some tongue-in-cheek "awards").

- Win a day off with pay.

- Casual dress days.

- Halloween costume day.

- Family picnics.

- World Series or football game pools (with prizes supplied by the company).

- Celebration of a local or civic event, company milestone, and so on.

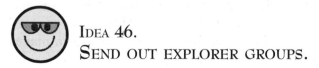

IDEA 46.
SEND OUT EXPLORER GROUPS.

When you hear about a great customer service idea another business is using, send out an exploration party to scope it out. Your employees will get a kick out of the excursion.

A supermarket known for exceptional service encourages employees to take a company van and rush to the scene of a good service idea used by another organization, including competitors. The employees take notes, discuss possible implementation in their store, and present their ideas to management.

USE MYSTERY SHOPPERS

Occasionally have employees explore the competition or similar businesses. Invite them to visit and fill out evaluation forms on what they observe, a process called mystery shopping. A sample evaluation form might look like the examples on pages 128 and 129.

You can customize a mystery shopper form to identify key factors or specific behaviors. You can also "explore" within your own company by having mystery shoppers visit your company's locations.

As a manager, be open to these ideas. Other companies do have good ideas and may often be doing things you could benefit from. Observe and build on their ideas. Send out your explorers.

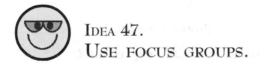

IDEA 47.
USE FOCUS GROUPS.

Focus groups have long been used for marketing research, but they can also play an exceptionally important role in understanding and managing customer expectations.

Although some marketing consultants may disagree with me, there's really no great mystery to how focus groups work, and any intelligent person could run one effectively.

SHOPPING FOR CONCERN, COMMUNICATION, AND COMPETENCE

Score each item below. Feel free to add comments. Use the following point system: 3 = superior; 2 = above standard; 1 = adequate; 0 = below standard; -1 = severely deficient; n/o = not observed.

Shopping for Concern

Company being evaluated: _____

Date & Time: _____

____1. The person serving me was appropriately dressed and neatly groomed.

____2. The person made eye contact with me quickly (within 10 seconds, preferably) when I approached him/her.

____3. The person focused on me, avoiding interruptions or distractions.

____4. The person used a timely and appropriate "ice breaker" to initiate conversation with me.

____5. Overall, the person made me feel comfortable.

Total:_____   **Average score:**_____

Comments about CONCERN experienced.
(Use other side as needed)

Shopping for Communication

___1. The person asked me about my specific needs.

___2. The person listened to me carefully.

___3. I was thanked for my business even if I didn't buy.

___4. The person called me by name or addressed me in a respectful manner.

___5. I felt the person was trying to establish accurate communication with me.

Total:_____   **Average score:**_____

Comments about COMMUNICATION experienced.
(Use other side as needed)

Shopping for Competence

___1. The person seemed competent in product knowledge.

___2. The person clarified my expectations about the products; cautioned me about limitations or misuse.

___3. Person suggested additional items I might want to purchase.

___4. Person explained features and benefits.

___5. Person followed up on commitments in a timely manner.

Total:_____   **Average score:**_____

Here is the procedure:

- Select a random sample of your customers (internal as well as external customers) to join with you in a feedback-sharing session. Don't pick just people you know or customers you like. You may, however, want to be sure that external customers are among your better customers by qualifying them according to how much they spend. You can get customer names off their checks or credit cards or whatever other records you have.

- Formally invite the customers to participate, telling them when and where as well as how long the session will take. Let them know the reason: that you are attempting to better understand customer needs and how you can better be of service to them.

- Keep your focus group to about a dozen people. Ask customers to confirm their attendance but expect that some will not show up. Fifteen confirmed reservations will generally get you twelve actual participants. If you use a mailed invitation, follow up with a phone call.

- Reward focus group participants. Tell those invited that you will give them something for their participation. Retail stores may give focus group participants a gift certificate, a free dinner, or even cash. In marketing research, it's not uncommon to pay people $50 dollars or more for a one- or two-hour session.

One supermarket I worked with was so excited about the focus groups that they invited 40 or 50 people every month! The problem, of course, is that a group that large makes it hard for all people to be heard. Some people dominated the group while others, who had equally good ideas but were uncomfortable speaking before so many people, suppressed their ideas.

To get the most from focus groups:

➥ Set the stage by having someone from top management moderate the group.

➥ Create an open atmosphere where participants will feel comfortable giving you all kinds of feedback. Be polite, open, encouraging, and receptive.

➥ Don't ever cut people off when they're making a critical comment, and do not, above all, be defensive of the way you're doing things now, when in the eyes of the customer it's not working.

➥ Apply the principle of naive listening. Keep any follow-up questions open-ended.

➥ When receiving compliments, make a statement such as, "Although we're happy to hear some compliments from you occasionally, our major purpose here is to identify ways that we can do a better job in meeting your needs." As focus group members express compliments, these should be acknowledged and thanked. However, the emphasis needs to be on where changes could be made to better meet the needs of the customers.

➥ Limit the group to a predetermined amount of time. People need to know how long they are expected to stay. Typically a one-hour or (maximum) 90-minute session works best. Any longer than that and you start losing people's interest.

➥ Tape record the entire focus group session and transcribe key notes for review. As you analyze the results of this group session, look for key words that might tip you off as to what the customers are looking for. If for example, concerns about the amount of time needed to complete their transaction comes up repeatedly, you might make the mental note of how can we best meet customer needs more quickly.

➥ At the end of the focus group session, of course, be sure to thank the participants for all of their input.

IDEA 48.
HANDLE TIME-WASTERS THAT DEFLECT
YOU FROM LOYALTY-BUILDING.

Following are five major time wasters with tips on how to avoid them.

TIME-WASTER #1: INTERRUPTIONS

Assertively decline to be interrupted. The next time someone asks, "Hey, got a minute?" you may be wise to gather up your most assertive skills and say, "Gosh, I really don't. I'm working on something for a customer right now. Could I get to you in about 20 minutes?"

Do you think anyone would be offended by an approach like that? It's unlikely. But even if they are, the appropriate use of your time is more important than their momentary pique. Occasionally offending overly sensitive people is a small price to pay for greater effectiveness and satisfaction.

The most important way of avoiding unproductive interruptions is simply to *decline to be interrupted.* Tell people that you're working on something right now and that you'd be glad to talk with them later.

Let people know when interruptions are okay. Schedule particular blocks of time that are open for people to come and visit you with their concerns. Scheduling such time and stick to those hours.

Respect other people's time. Don't interrupt others unless absolutely necessary. Always check with people to be sure they are not in the middle of a high-priority activity, such as dealing with customer needs. When calling on the phone ask, "Do you have a minute to talk about this now?" before launching into the topic of your call. By doing so, you send another unspoken message that you value time—theirs and your own.

TIME-WASTER #2: UNPRODUCTIVE COMMUNICATION

Choose the right media for your message. Don't send a letter when a phone call will do. Don't make a call when a personal visit is needed (even if the visit takes more time and energy). Communication efficiency is simply a matter of "reaching" the most people at the lowest cost. Memos, posters, and mass meetings can do that. Communication effectiveness, however, means reaching the right people with the right message in a timely and useful form. Often this means one-to-one conversation with customers and employees, small group discussions, and the like. Effective communication media almost always costs more than efficient media if used inappropriately (such as a mass announcement of an issue that should have been personally).

TIME-WASTER #3: CLUTTER AND PAPERWORK

Handle each paper only once. Learn to make decisions—don't just postpone action—on each letter, memo, or document you receive.

Usually you have four options:

F File it for future reference.
R Refer it to someone else.
A Act on it—now!
T Trash it.

Studies show that 95 percent of the stuff in files for more than one year will never be used. Periodically clean out those files so that your system stays lean and efficient. When in doubt, throw it out. Get a handle on the kinds of information you need to keep and get rid of the rest. Don't get bogged down in sheer quantity of stuff cluttering your life.

TIME-WASTER #4: PROCRASTINATION

Nothing impresses so significantly as immediate follow-up. Customers and employees will be impressed with you if you avoid procrastination and, as the shoe commercial says, "just do it!"

Some experts say there are just three reasons for procrastination: fear of failure, fear of success, or the desire to rebel against "the system." Determine which reason you are using when you procrastinate a task. Then, try these tips:

- *Use a daily priority task list.* Prioritize your work for each day and use some form of a planner.

- *Do the worst task first.* Get it over with and enjoy the rest of the day.

- *Make dreaded tasks into games.* Compete against others or yourself. Try to beat your last effort. Play mind games.

- *Discipline.* Sorry, but ultimately it may come down to that.

TIME-WASTER #5: INDECISION

Avoid indecision with the simple three-word motto, READY-FIRE-AIM. Think through your idea (get ready), try it (fire!), and observe/correct the results as needed (aim). Wal-Mart founder Sam Walton used this approach when he constantly challenged his people to try out new ideas, not just mull them over in their minds. Get yourself *doing something* and then adjust the aim as necessary.

Also avoid "perfection paralysis." Everything you do won't be right, but start with a "rough draft" and shape and improve as you go.

IDEA 49.
APPLY THE FOUR R'S FOR CONSISTENT GROWTH.

Four major components are useful to bring about consistent progress. This principle applies to customer loyalty building as well as other aspects of our lives. These Four R's are also found in all major religions. Think about their applicability to your efforts in serving customers.

R #1—RITUALS

In religions, these are the ceremonies that we regularly observe to remind ourselves of significant religious truths. In building customer loyalty, they are our routine activities to advance us toward desired goals and values. Daily actions such as personal and workplace appearance, habits of thanking and complementing customers, prompt and personal greetings, and an overall commitment to regular behaviors needed to build customer loyalty are examples of such rituals.

R #2—RESTRICTIONS

In religions, these are the prohibitions that instruct us in what to avoid. In customer loyalty building, they are also the limits beyond which you decide you will not trespass. For example, you make a commitment that you will not associate with an organization that employs unethical or shady practices, or you will not cut ethical corners for the sake of short-term customer advantage. The process of stating the organizational taboos (in Idea 37) is a clear example of the second R.

R #3—REGULATIONS

In religions, these are the commandments that encourage us to do positive acts, such as honoring our parents, contributing to the needy, attending services, and loving our neighbors. In building customer loyalty, the regulations are our guidelines for valuing customers, our commitment to building long-term relationships with them, to giving A-plus service, and to being fair and honest in all our dealings. These regulations need to be value congruent with the company credo and the commitment to excellence for employees, customers, and other stakeholders.

R #4—RELATIONSHIPS

The outcome of the first three R's affects the fourth. We become more caring for others as we grow and succeed. We

recognize that little can be accomplished without the coopera-
tion and help of others. We recognize the value of relationships in our personal and organizational success. In the long
run, no accomplishment can compensate for destroyed relationships. Relationships are the ultimate end of our existence,
for we are commanded above all to love one another.

So, at the risk of sounding a bit preachy, I ask that you
consider these four R's and how they can impact any ongoing
loyalty-building efforts.

PART VI

THE 50 POWERFUL IDEAS SUMMARIZED

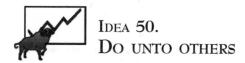

IDEA 50.
DO UNTO OTHERS

The Bible teaches the most succinct summary of all these *50 powerful ideas:*

> *Therefore all things whatsoever ye would have that men should do to you, do ye even so to them.*

Matthew 7:12

I hope you'll reread these 50 powerful ideas and use them starting today. You will experience greater fulfillment and success in all that you do.

BONUS SECTION:
A STEP-BY-STEP PLAN FOR IMPLEMENTING A
CUSTOMER LOYALTY STRATEGY

An application guide to translating slogans
and good intentions into workable strategy

The following pages describe a step-by-step process for implementing and sustaining ongoing customer loyalty efforts. A customer loyalty strategy invites all employees to consistently participate and impact the organization's bottom line.

CRITICAL ELEMENTS NEEDED FOR ANY APPROACH TO WORK

Any successful approach to enhancing customer loyalty must begin with these criteria:

1. Top Management Support. The amount of enthusiasm demonstrated by management will reflect throughout the organization. Managers at all levels must buy into the effort and communicate supportiveness to employees at all levels. If top management is not 100 percent committed, the overall effort will not succeed.

2. Training and Motivation. Dynamic, interesting training sessions are needed to provide information and skills-building opportunities. These should be structured in such a way as to help employees see "what's in this for them," create the excitement, and reinforce a commitment needed for ongoing success.

3. Employee Involvement and Empowerment. Staff at all levels of the company need to be encouraged to participate. A "top-down" process of management dictates does not work. Management cannot simply demand certain behaviors and expect employees to participate with enthusiasm.

Involve people of all organizational levels via:

- Soliciting their suggestions (and rewarding them for suggesting).
- Involving them in brainstorming sessions.
- Inviting them to participate in focus groups and explorer teams.
- Acknowledging and reinforcing service excellence.

STARTING POINT: AGREEMENT ON A PHILOSOPHY

Seek agreement on the importance of ongoing loyalty-building efforts by teaching and reminding employees of these critical facts:

- Building customer loyalty must be Job 1.

- Loyal customers impact an organization's bottom line more than any ad campaign or public relations effort.

- It costs at least five times as much to generate a new customer than to keep an existing one.

- Dissatisfied customers produce devastating ripple effects through negative word-of-mouth "advertising."

- The cost of the lost customer quickly dissipates any benefits gained through community relations, advertising, or marketing taken alone.

- Companies can best build loyalty by exceeding customer expectations.

- Internal customer (employee) relations are a critical part of the loyalty-building process.

- Long-term, incremental improvements add a dynamic quality to the strategy and breathe life into the process.

Review Part 1 of this book: Powerful Ideas That Get You Focused.

ASSIGN A LEADERSHIP TEAM

Put together a team of associates who have good customer skills. Assign them the task of championing the efforts to build loyalty. Give them resources needed to launch and sustain your efforts. Among the resources they may need are:

- Time away from their other work responsibilities.
- Access to training. Send them to seminars or conferences on customer loyalty.
- Books, subscriptions for further research.
- Budget money to pay for focus groups, explorer groups, employee incentives.
- Facilities for meeting and training.
- Access to employee groups.

Use people from various organizational areas and levels. Make their selection a special honor, not just extra work. When selecting people, look for these qualifications:

- Excellent customer attitudes.
- Demonstrated skills in handling customer issues.
- Creativity and enthusiasm.
- Shared vision of what the company is trying to accomplish.
- Good communication skills.
- Initiative and willingness to take reasonable risk.
- A track record for accomplishment.

Keep the team to a manageable size. Teams of three to seven members seem to work best. Let the team be self-managed. Give them your input about what you'd like to see happen, but then back off. Do not micro-manage. Let them come up with ideas and approaches.

CREATE AND MAINTAIN ENTHUSIASM

Perhaps the most serious mistake companies make in implementing customer loyalty strategy efforts is to convey to employees that this constitutes a new *program* or *campaign*. It is crucial to stress from the very beginning, that building customer loyalty is not a *program* but rather an *ongoing philosophy*—a way the company will be doing business over the long term.

The challenges facing the organization as it initiates a customer satisfaction strategy are to:

1. *Convince employees* that management is serious about consistent improvement in customer loyalty and that management's emphasis is not a passing fad or empty slogan. Show that the organization will provide resources to make the strategy work.

2. *Provide the tools employees need* in the form of additional training and motivation to apply and use the techniques of customer loyalty building.

3. *Create* or *modify reward systems* to support the strategy. (Review Idea 35.)

4. Create *consistency of emphasis* on the strategy so that you dispel the illusions that "this too shall pass."

5. *Supply employees with the expertise* they need to solve customer problems or challenges. Use outside experts as needed.

6. *Publicize the loyalty-building efforts* so that various stakeholders (customers, potential customers, employees, the community, shareholders) are aware of the results.

7. *Empower and involve all company personnel* in the evolution and growth of the strategy. (Review Idea 34.)

IMPLEMENT AN APPROACH

The following outlines a systematic approach for implementing a successful customer loyalty strategy. This approach is based on proven procedures I've developed over many years of serving companies. It reflects a theoretically sound and highly practical way of translating current thinking on customer loyalty into a workable plan of action.

I strongly recommend that you not be tempted by a "canned" program offered by some consultants or training firms. These do not produce long-term results. The strategy developed within your company must be uniquely applicable to your organization's people and culture.

Implementation involves three major phases:

1. Strategic planning and needs assessment.
2. Training and motivation (managers first, then staff).
3. Continuation support (including follow-up training).

THREE PHASES OF A TYPICAL STRATEGY IMPLEMENTATION

The table on pages 144 and 145 shows the three major phases of a typical strategy. The requirements of both the leadership team and the organization are shown. (*Note*: These are not in chronological order. Some activities overlap.)

The involvement of the leadership team will vary over time. Early in the implementation, they would be more heavily involved. As the strategy becomes integrated into the company culture, their efforts will be lessened.

One final thought: Perhaps the most important aspect of this strategy development process is to make customer loyalty an ongoing priority, not just a "program."

A-Plus thinking forms the basis for a strategy, not just a slogan. (Review especially Ideas 22-25) If you're not thinking A-Plus, your competition may be.

LEADERSHIP TEAM RESPONSIBILITY	COMPANY RESPONSIBILITY
Phase 1: Strategic Planning and Needs Assessment	
• Needs assessment (employee focus groups to determine concerns about giving service and training needed) • Pre-testing—measure current results using CLI (see Idea 44) • Determination of objectives; clarify goals • Analysis of company customer data and/or customer focus groups	• Participation and support • Employees gather customer loyalty data • Participation of manager most involved with implementation (the program champions) • Access to data or arranged focus group participants
Phase 2: Training and Motivation	

• Manager's retreat and strategy launch to preview the approach recommended by team
• Distribute books; provide training sessions (see Idea 36) for all employees that includes:
  • Importance of customer loyalty
  • Attitudes toward serving
  • Communication skills
  • "A-Plus" customer loyalty
  • Buy-in activities
	• Managers (off site location)
	• All employees (including managers) attend sessions on company time or compensated for after-hours

LEADERSHIP TEAM RESPONSIBILITY	COMPANY RESPONSIBILITY
Phase 3: Continuation Support (Follow-up)	
• Post-testing. Repeat Customer Loyalty Index (Idea 44) and score • Mail-outs to line managers on a regular basis • Non-mandatory training sessions on related topics for reinforcement (Idea 36) • Assist in developing reward program (Idea 35) • Regular repeats on training sessions for new hires • Materials for company newsletter and/or press releases • Encourage the hiring of people who have good attitudes toward customers—people who have been seen dealing well with customers (Idea 39)	• Employees gather customer data • Publicize and encourage attendance • Create A-Plus rewards system and celebrations (see Ideas 35, 45) • Provide newsletter/press release channels • Maintain file of potential employees

PART I.

[1] These feedback ideas are adapted from Joe Folkman's *Making Feedback Work* (Provo, UT: Novations Group, Inc., 1998), p. 123.

[2] These Office of Consumer Affairs statistics are quoted in *The Customer Service Manager's Handbook of People Power Strategies* (Englewood Cliffs, NJ: Prentice-Hall, Inc., 1989), p. 3.

[3] Jonah Keri, "Satisfaction, Profits Fly Hand in Hand," *Investor's Business Daily*, January 30, 2001, p. 1.

[4] All names are fictitious. If there is a "Happy Jack's Supermarket" somewhere, it's not the one described in this story.

[5] Many argue that with the prevalence of easy communication available in the information age, the "six-times-as-much" figure is too low. People broadcast the bad news more widely than ever and customers become even more hesitant to visit a business others have had problems with.

[6] The concept of "A-Plus" presented here is adapted from Paul R. Timm, *Seven Power Strategies for Building Customer Loyalty* (New York: AMACOM, 2001), Chapter 4.

[7] Timm, Paul R., "Effects of Inequity in Supervisory Communication Behavior on Subordinates in Clerical Workgroups," Florida State University, 1977. Unpublished doctoral dissertation.

PART II.

[1] Some of this material adapted from Sherron Bienvenu and Paul R. Timm, *Business Communication: Discovering Strategy, Developing Skills* (Upper Saddle River, NJ: Prentice Hall, Inc., 2002), Chapter 11.

[2] See S. Bienvenu Kenton and D. Valentine, *CrossTalk: Communicating in a Multicultural Workplace* (Upper Saddle River, NJ: Prentice-Hall, Inc., 1997)

[3] "That's Retailtainment," *Wal-Mart Annual Report 2001*, p. 7.

[4] See Richard B. Chase, and Sriram Dasu, "Want to Perfect Your Company's Service? Use Behavioral Science," *Harvard Business Review*, June 2001, pp. 79-84.

PART III.

[1] "Common Threads," in *Inc.* magazine, August 2001, p. 51.

[2] See Richard B. Chase, and Sriram Dasu, "Want to Perfect Your Company's Service? Use Behavioral Science," *Harvard Business Review*, June 2001, pp. 79-84.

[3] Ibid, p. 81.

[4] Michael Janofsky, "RV Drivers 'Camp' at Wal-Mart," *New York Times News Service*, July 27, 2001.

[5] Thomas G. Stemberg, "My Biggest Mistake," *Inc.*, August 2001, p. 75.

[6] "Valet-parking demand surges, but parking can cause headaches," *Wall Street Journal*, August 21, 2001, p. A-1.

PART IV.

[1] Scott Carlson, "More Colleges Offer Graduates Lifetime E-Mail Addresses," *The Chronicle of Higher Education*, August 17, 2001, p. A29.

² Adapted from "How to Deal with Those Chronic Complainers," in *Customer Service Manager's Letter*, September 20, 1989. Published by Prentice-Hall Professional Newsletters. The article is based on the work of Dr. Robert Bramson, *Coping with Difficult People* (New York: Dell, 1988).

PART IV.

¹ See Timothy W. Firnstahl, "My Employees Are My Service Guarantee," *Harvard Business Review*, July-August 1989, pp. 28-32.

² Written by Susan Feldman, Editor-in-Chief, *Investment Vision,* a publication of Fidelity Investments.

³ From "The Smart Sales Staff," published in *Success,* April 1989.

⁴ From Jack Weissman Associates as quoted in *Customer Service Manager's Letter*, (a Prentice-Hall Professional Newsletter), September 6, 1989.

⁵ This measure of customer loyalty is a simplified form based on findings of the Gallup polling organization. See *Gallup Management Magazine*, Summer 2001.

H
Hoopla and fun, 125-126

I
Icons, 91
Inc. magazine, 83
Inequity, 37-40
Insults,
   gender, 53
   racial, 53
   religious, 53
Interview, good,
   characteristics of, 47-48
Involvement, depth of, 49-50

J
Job factors, 121
Jobs, enrich people's, 117

K
Keri, Jonah, 23

L
Layout, 91
Listen, 66-67, 97
Listener, be a better, 21-22
Loyalty, 15

M
Media, use a different, 78
Motivate, 33

N
Naïve listening, 73
Name-calling, 64-65
Needs, anticipate customer,
   67-68
Negative feedback, fish for, 73
Non-verbal behaviors, 50
Note-taking skills, 67
Nurture caring, 115-116

O
Objective 33
   standards, 34
Opportunist, 66

P
Packaging, 74
People turnoffs, 17
Perceived expectations, 33
Peters, Tom, 106
Please and thank you, 62-63
Price, 33
Profanity, 53
Public Relations, 7

Dr. Paul R. Timm is one of America's foremost experts on customer loyalty. He has written 38 books and scores of articles on customer service, human relations, communication, and self-management. He holds a doctorate degree from Florida State University in organizational communication and is a professor of Management Communication in the Marriott School of Management at Brigham Young University. He also teaches in the executive MBA program at the Helsinki School of Economics and Business Administration in Finland.

As an active consultant and trainer, Timm has worked with thousands of people from organizations throughout North America and Europe. He wrote and appears in eight video-tape training programs sold worldwide, including *The Power of Customer Service, Successful Self-Management,* and the tape program based on this book, *50 Ways to Keep Your Customers (and Get New Ones)*. These videos are produced by JWA Video of Chicago; call 312-829-5100 or e-mail JWAVideo@aol.com for information.

Among Timm's books are the popular Career Press title *50 Ways to Win New Customers* and *Seven Power Strategies for Building Customer Loyalty* from AMACOM Publishing.

Paul Timm encourages reader comments and can be reached via e-mail at DrTimm@aol.com

YOUR FEEDBACK IS APPRECIATED

Please e-mail any comments about this book to the above address. I really want to know how you like my book and how I could serve you better. Thank you for reading this and my best wishes for building customer loyalty in your organization.

— Paul R. Timm

Dr. Paul R. Timm will be happy to help you with customer loyalty training and consulting. For further information or to arrange an organizational assessment, contact Dr. Timm at DrTimm@aol.com.

TOF

- WWLO
- WWC
- OAS
- Constant Cont
- HF
- YHA
- Seminars